GW00601583

Smart Guide to

Microsoft®
Office 2000

Smart Guide to

Microsoft®
Office 2000

Stephen L. Nelson

NET.WORKS

The company and product names used in this book are the trademarks
or registered trademarks of their respective owners.

Copyright © 1998 by Stephen L. Nelson, Inc.

This edition published by Net.Works, P O Box 200, Harrogate, N. Yorks. HG1 2YR
England

Net.Works is an imprint of Take That Ltd

Published by arrangement with Barnes & Noble, Inc.

All rights reserved. No part of this book may be used or reproduced in
any manner whatsoever without the written permission of the Publisher.

ISBN 1-873668-77-5

Printed and bound in the United States of America

99 00 01 M 9 8 7 6 5 4 3 2 1

FG

Contents

INTRODUCTION

None of us want to linger in a book's Introduction. We want to get on with it, begin reading the important stuff, and begin getting answers to questions. Nevertheless, let me suggest that you take time to read or at least skim this Introduction. It briefly discusses the following important topics related to Microsoft Office:

- A brief history of Office
- What is Office?
- What's new in Office 2000?
- How to use this Smart Guide
- Assumptions about you
- Conventions used here

With this important background information, you'll find it easier to understand why Office works the way it does and how you can get the most value from this book.

A Brief History of Office

A discussion of the history of Office may seem irrelevant, but in fact it's very useful. A review actually puts several points in perspective.

Not so very long ago, Microsoft wasn't a dominant developer of application software. (Application software simply describes the programs that let you do word-processing or build spreadsheets and so forth.) Microsoft was the major developer of operating system software. It made and sold the MS-DOS and Microsoft Windows operating systems. A different company made the best-selling word-processing program, WordPerfect. Another company made the best-selling spreadsheet program, Lotus 1-2-3. And yet another company made the best-selling database program.

Microsoft certainly made good application software. But computer users are, if anything, a pragmatic bunch. Users happy with one program just weren't inclined to try something new. And that was true even if the something new was a bit better: easier to use, more powerful, or less expensive.

Microsoft dealt with the challenge of motivating people to purchase its application software in a pretty clever way. Borrowing a successful concept from novelty retailers, Microsoft created a grab bag product. It took its word-processor program, its spreadsheet program, and several other programs as well, put them together into the same box, and sold them all for essentially the same price that its competitors sold an individual program. The grab bag concept—which Microsoft labeled a "suite" of programs—took off. People—and especially people in large corporations—found themselves asking, "Should I pay $500 for a word processor or $500 for a whole suite of programs that includes a word processor?" The obvious answer was "I'll take the suite."

People loved the economics of the grab bag. And not very many months later, Microsoft's application software had become the dominant programs in most of the major application categories.

What Is Office?

The preceding sketch of Microsoft Office's history helps you more easily make sense of the Office product. For example, you can instantly grasp the point that the Office product can be packaged in combinations that differ from one box to the next. (Microsoft actually sells several different versions of its popular grab bag.) And you can understand the point that you don't actually do anything with Office itself. You work with the individual programs that make up the Office suite. Finally, you can more easily make sense of Office's richness if you understand that Office is still, essentially, a grab bag of individual programs.

So which individual programs make up the Office suite? Microsoft assembles the Office product by putting some combination of the following programs into the box:

- Microsoft Word, a word processor you use to create and publish text documents. This book describes Word in Chapters 3 and 4.

- Microsoft Excel, a spreadsheet program you use to perform numerical analysis, including budgeting, forecasting, and financial analysis. This book describes Excel in Chapter 5.

- Microsoft Outlook, a personal information manager you use to send and receive e-mail, maintain a contacts list, keep your calendar, and perform several other time-management tasks as well. This book describes Outlook in Chapters 6 and 7.

- Microsoft Internet Explorer, a web browser you use to view and work with Internet resources such as web pages. This book describes Internet Explorer in Chapter 8.

- Microsoft PowerPoint, a presentation program you use to create electronic slide shows such as you might use in formal sales presentations. This book describes PowerPoint in Chapter 9.

- Microsoft Publisher, a desktop publishing program you use to create publications such as newsletters, brochures, and even books. This book describes Publisher in Chapter 10.

- Microsoft Access, a database program you use to collect, store, and manage rich sets of information such as employee records, inventory information, and membership lists. This book describes Access in Chapter 11.

- Microsoft FrontPage, a web authoring program you use to create web pages and administer web sites.

- Microsoft PhotoDraw, an illustration program you use to create digital art, including graphic images used on web pages.

- Microsoft Small Business Solutions, a collection of tools especially useful for small and growing businesses, including one tool that lets you extract information from an accounting program and then analyze it in a special Excel spreadsheet and another tool that lets you more easily manage direct-mail campaigns.

 FrontPage, PhotoDraw, and Small Business Solutions are not described in this book.

Microsoft combines these building blocks in several ways to create different versions of Office, as Table I-1 indicates. The most popular versions of the Office bundle are the Standard version, which includes Word, Excel, Outlook, Internet Explorer, and PowerPoint, and the Professional version, which includes everything in the Standard version plus Access and Publisher.

Program	Standard	Professional	Small Business	Enterprise
Word	Yes	Yes	Yes	Yes
Excel	Yes	Yes	Yes	Yes
Outlook	Yes	Yes	Yes	Yes
Internet Explorer	Yes	Yes	Yes	Yes
PowerPoint	Yes	Yes	No	Yes
Access	No	Yes	No	Yes
Publisher	No	Yes	Yes	Yes
FrontPage	No	No	No	Yes
PhotoDraw	No	No	No	Yes
Small Business Solutions and Small Business Bookshelf	No	Yes	Yes	Yes

TABLE I-1: Typical components of different versions of Office.

 The Professional and Premier versions of Office contain other tools in addition to the major programs listed in Table I-1. Both versions will probably include the Office Web Components, for example. Chapter 8 briefly describes the Office Web Components and how they work.

What's New in Office 2000?

Microsoft updates the Office suite roughly every two years, adding new features to the individual programs. Sometimes the new features amount to little more than bells and whistles. Other times, they provide terrific new tools that we can exploit to do more with our computers.

Office 2000's new features fall into the latter category. The three major categories of new features in Office 2000—adaptability, installation logic, and web awareness—greatly expand our opportunities.

Adaptability

The adaptability feature is the first thing you'll notice about working with the new Office programs. As the Office programs have evolved over the years, the menus and toolbars have become more and more cluttered. If you're someone who uses all of a program's features, this clutter might not bother you. However, most people don't use all of a program's features, so as the number of menus and commands grows, and as the toolbars contain ever greater numbers of buttons and boxes, most people just get frustrated. Finding a menu command or toolbar button has become a bit like looking for a needle in a haystack.

The developers at Microsoft recognized this problem and came up with a couple of solutions: personal menus and personal toolbars. A personal menu displays only those commands you regularly use or are likely to use, and the Personal toolbar displays only those buttons and boxes that you regularly use or are likely to use. The process of creating personal menus and toolbars takes a couple of weeks of using the programs, but they can greatly simplify your work. Take a look at Figure I-1, which shows a full menu, and compare it to Figure I-2, which shows a personal version of it. The fewer number of commands on the personal menu makes the Office program much easier to use.

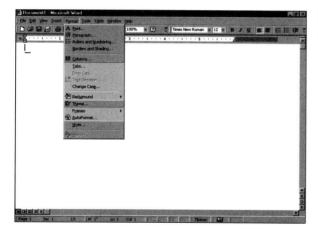

FIGURE I-1

The full Word Format menu.

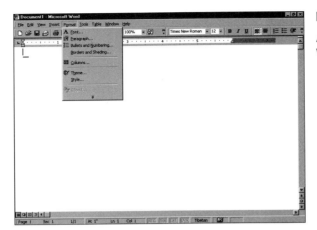

FIGURE I-2

A personal-menu version of Word's Format menu.

 You don't lose access to the full command set by working with personal menus. You can display the full menu of an Office program by clicking the double-chevrons at the bottom of the menu or by simply holding the menu open.

The same sort of evolution has occurred with the two toolbars that most Office programs used to provide. Figure I-3 shows the Word program window with the traditional Standard and Formatting toolbars displayed. (The toolbars are those two rows of buttons that appear beneath the menu bar.) Figure I-4 shows the Word program window with the new Personal toolbar. The Personal toolbar combines the most frequently used tools from the Standard and Formatting toolbars, making it easier for users—that's you and me—to work with an Office program.

 You don't lose access to the full toolbar tool set by working with the Personal toolbar. You can display a list of the other toolbar tools of an Office program by clicking the double chevrons on the Personal toolbar. When you click the double chevrons, the Office program displays a pop-up box of buttons. When you click a button, you choose it, and the Office program adds the button to the Personal toolbar.

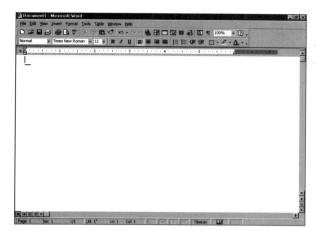

FIGURE I-3

The Word program window with the traditional Standard and Formatting toolbars displayed.

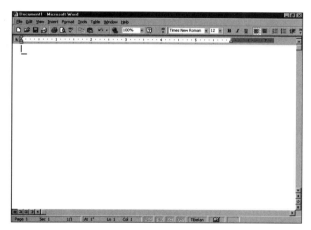

FIGURE I-4

The Word program window with the Personal toolbar.

Notes *You can reconfigure your personal menus and toolbars for an Office program. To do this, choose the Tools menu's Customize command, click the Options tab, and then click Reset My Usage Data.*

Intelligent Installation and Install on Demand

A second big feature new to Office 2000 relates to its installation, or setup, program. The Office setup program is now intelligent enough that it installs only those Office components you're likely to use. (The setup program makes these determinations by looking at your computer and any older versions of Office you've used.) And that makes installing Office easier. (Appendix A describes how to install Office 2000.)

The Office setup program also now installs any missing or corrupted components as it needs them. For example, perhaps the Office setup program didn't install a particular component of the Office program originally. Or suppose that a piece of the Office program gets corrupted or is somehow deleted. Office now automatically requests the setup program to install the missing or corrupted piece. If the setup program can find the missing piece—say, you're working on a network—it just goes and grabs the missing piece from the network. If the setup program can't find the missing piece, it requests that you insert the Office CD-ROM, so it can retrieve the missing piece from the disc.

These new installation features are very useful because you don't have to devote time to figuring out which pieces of the Office suite of programs you need to install, reinstall, or replace. Office does this work for you.

Web Awareness

Perhaps the most exciting set of new features in Office 2000 relates to web awareness. Office 2000 programs see the Internet and internal web servers (such as might be used on an intranet) as tools for sharing Office documents. This new perspective makes a big difference to anybody who works on the Internet or an intranet.

For example, Office 2000 programs now use **HTML** as an alternate file format for Office documents. This means that Office documents can easily be stored on web servers and then read by people with access to the web server and a web browser.

 Notes *A web browser is a program such as Internet Explorer 5 or Netscape Navigator that lets you read a web page.*

If Office documents are stored on a web server running the Office Server Extensions software, you can use Office programs to collaborate on an Office document. You could, for example, make changes to an Office document at the same time that another person is making changes and a third person is reading the document.

Some of the Office programs—notably Excel, Access, and PowerPoint—let you create Web Components. A Web Component is just a portion of an Office document that can be placed in a web page and then viewed and even edited using a web browser such as Internet Explorer 5.

How to Use This Smart Guide

If you're brand new to Office and want to learn everything you can in as short a time as possible, then you should read this book from start to finish. But if you've worked with an Office program a little in the past, you might want to skip around in the book. You might not need to read Chapters 1 and 2, for example. Instead, you might want to read a chapter that describes a program you haven't yet used.

You can also use this book as a reference for those times when you're stuck or are scratching your head about how to accomplish a task or work with an Office feature. Just turn to the table of contents or the index to look up the topic that's causing you trouble. Then you can dip right in, read a few paragraphs to answer your questions, and get back to work. This book is written in a way that allows you to read it using all of these techniques.

Assumptions About You

As I wrote this book, I had to make a few assumptions about your computer skills and knowledge. I tried to make this book apply to the widest range of people and experiences as I possibly could. However, people use several different versions of the Office suite, they perform a wide variety of tasks with the programs, and they also possess varying degrees of knowledge about computers and software. In a little book such as this one, there's just not room to describe all the different ways that people with different computer skills can accomplish various tasks in every version of Office.

This book assumes you're working with either the Standard or Professional version of Office. (See Table I-1 for a description of what these two popular versions of Office include.) Word and Outlook, the two most commonly used Office programs, are covered extensively, with two chapters each. Excel, Internet Explorer, and PowerPoint, are thoroughly discussed in individual chapters. Access and Publisher are also described in single, yet smaller, chapters.

 Chapters 1 and 2 present information you'll find useful in working with all the Office programs. Chapter 1, for example, explains how to start and stop Office programs and how to save and open documents. Chapter 2 explains how to carry out several tasks that are common to each of the Office programs.

Although this book introduces computing terminology and steps you through some complex tasks, it is designed to be useful to people who have never before worked with Office programs. If you're a beginner, you don't need any special computer or Windows knowledge to use *Smart Guide to Microsoft Office 2000*. If you've worked with Office programs and consider yourself an intermediate user, you can use *Smart Guide to Microsoft Office 2000* to expand or refresh your skills.

 You'll find it helpful to know some Windows basics before you begin reading. For example, you should know how to start and stop programs, choose commands, and work with dialog boxes. If you need to learn these skills, you might want to look for the **Smart Guide to Windows 98.**

Conventions Used Here

This book uses some simple conventions for presenting information. When I want to share a tidbit of information that is relative to the topic at hand but interrupts the flow of discussion, I'll set that information apart with an icon in the margin.

 A Note provides backup or additional information that relates to the general discussion but isn't critical to your understanding. A Note is also used to point out exceptions for special situations.

 A Tip offers advice or presents information that can save you time and trouble.

 A Warning alerts you to potential trouble spots or mistakes easily made.

From here on out, whenever you see a **boldface** term, it means that term is defined in the Glossary. A Glossary term is set in boldface the first time it's used in a chapter. For example, if the term **operating system** is used in a discussion and you don't know what an operating system is, you can flip back to the Glossary and look it up.

CHAPTER 1

Getting Started with Office

To get started working with Microsoft Office 2000, you'll need to know how to accomplish several important tasks. This chapter describes how to perform the following tasks that are common to almost all the Office **programs:**

- Starting Office programs
- Creating new **documents**
- Opening documents
- Saving documents
- Saving documents as **web pages**
- Importing and exporting documents
- Closing documents
- Exiting Office programs
- Getting help within Office

Starting Office Programs

Most Office programs start in the same way. To start a program, follow these steps:

1 **Click** the Start button.

2 Point to Programs to display a list of the programs you have on your computer, as shown in Figure 1-1.

3 Click the program you want to start.

 Notes **Microsoft Internet Explorer 5's** *component programs may not appear directly on the Programs menu, but instead in the Internet Explorer* **folder** *on the Programs menu.*

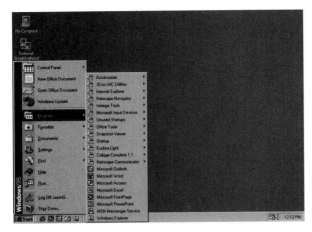

FIGURE 1-1

The Programs menu.

You can also start Office programs in two other, faster ways. First, you can start a program by **double-clicking** its icon on the desktop, as shown in Figure 1-2. Office programs don't automatically create desktop icons when you install them, but it's a good idea to do this yourself for the programs you use most frequently. Refer to the **Microsoft Windows** documentation for information about how to do this. Second, if you're using Internet Explorer 4 or later or Windows 98, you can start Internet Explorer and **Microsoft Outlook Express** by clicking their buttons on the Quick Launch toolbar, which is located next to the Start button, probably at the bottom of your screen.

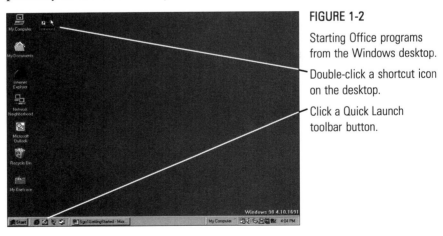

FIGURE 1-2

Starting Office programs from the Windows desktop.

Double-click a shortcut icon on the desktop.

Click a Quick Launch toolbar button.

Creating New Documents

Typically, when you start an Office program, the program creates a new blank document for you. If you start **Microsoft Word 2000**, for example, Word creates a blank document named Document1 and displays this blank document in the Word **program window**, as shown in Figure 1-3.

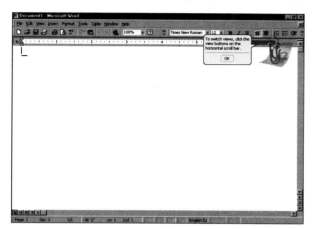

FIGURE 1-3

Word creates a new blank document when it starts.

However, you can also tell an Office program to create a new document. To create a new document in most Office programs, choose the File **menu's** New command. Often when you choose this command, the program opens a **dialog box** in which you specify the type of document you want to create. For example, Figure 1-4 shows the dialog box Word displays when you choose the File menu's New command.

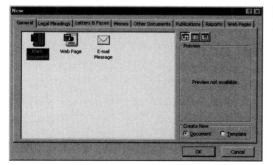

FIGURE 1-4

The New dialog box in Word.

*Different Office programs create different documents. Word creates text documents such as letters, memos, and reports. **Microsoft Excel 2000** creates **spreadsheet** documents, called **workbooks**, to use for budgets, forecasts, and other tabular presentations of numeric data. Some Office programs run a **wizard** when they start and running the wizard creates the new document. **Microsoft Access 2000, Microsoft PowerPoint 2000,** and **Microsoft Publisher 2000** work in this way.*

New dialog boxes for Office programs often allow you to select the template on which you want to base your new document. A template is a blank document that contains formatting, blocks of stock text, or predesigned elements.

 *Office programs also include a button on the **toolbar** for creating a new document. This button usually creates a document based on the default template.*

Opening Documents

To open documents in an Office program, you can use one of two ways. You can open documents from Windows, just as you can other **files** or programs, or you can open documents from within an Office program.

Opening an Office Document with Windows

You can open existing Office documents from Windows. If you click a document listed on the Documents menu, Windows starts the program you used to create the document and then tells it to open the document. For example, if you see a Word document listed in the Documents menu, clicking this document starts Word and opens the document.

 To find the Documents menu, click the Start button and then point to Documents.

Another easy way to open an Office document is by using My Computer or Windows Explorer. If you double-click an Office document listed in the My Computer or Windows Explorer window, Windows starts the program you used to create the document and then tells it to open the document.

Notes To open the My Computer window, double-click the My Computer icon, which appears on the Windows desktop. To start Windows Explorer, click the Start button, point to Programs, and then click Windows Explorer. For information on how to use the My Computer window or Windows Explorer, refer to the Windows documentation or a general Windows reference, such as the Smart Guide to Windows 98.

Opening an Office Document with Office

You can also open Office documents from within Office programs. In other words, you can first start an Office program like Word and then use Word to open the document you want to work with. Typically you choose the File menu's Open command to display a dialog box similar to the one shown in Figure 1-5.

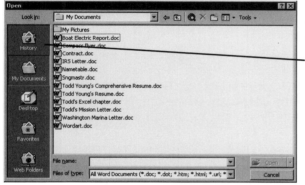

FIGURE 1-5

The Open dialog box in Word.

The Places bar.

To use this dialog box, follow these steps:

1 If the document you want to open is one you've recently used or one that is stored in a location represented by the buttons on the **Places bar,** click History, My Documents, Desktop, **Favorites,** or **Web Folders** to locate the document.

- History displays a list of documents you've previously opened or saved.

- My Documents displays the contents of the My Documents folder.

- Desktop displays a list of the documents you've stored on the Windows Desktop.

- Favorites displays a list of the documents you've added to your Favorites list.
- Web Folders displays a list of web servers you might have used to store a document.

2 If the document you want to open isn't stored in a location represented by the buttons on the Places bar, use the Look In drop-down list box to select the drive where the document is located. Then, locate the folder that contains the document in the large list box. Double-click the folder to view its contents.

 *You might need to repeat the last part of step 2 if the document you want to open is stored in a **subfolder** of another folder.*

3 Click the document you want to open to select it.

4 Click Open.

 If you accidentally try to open a document you already have opened, the program might ask if you want to revert to the saved version of the document. Unless you want to lose the changes you've made to the document, click No to cancel opening the document.

Saving Documents

In general, Office programs don't save documents after every change you make. For example, you need to tell Office programs such as Word, Excel, or PowerPoint to save a document.

 Word and Excel might automatically save documents periodically. However, you should still save your work as well, just as a precaution. It's a good idea to save a document at least once every half hour. Then, if the power should go out or your program or computer should crash, the most you lose is a half hour's worth of work.

To save a document, follow these steps:

1 Choose the File menu's Save command. If this is the first time you've saved the document, the program displays a dialog box similar to the one shown in Figure 1-6. You use this dialog box to name the document, specify a document type, and select a location to store the document.

FIGURE 1-6

The Save As dialog box.

The Create New Folder toolbar button.

2 Click the History, My Documents, Desktop, Favorites, or Web Folders button on the Places bar to save the document to a common location.

- History displays a list of documents you've recently saved. (Use this button when you want to replace a previously saved document with the new document.)

- My Documents opens the My Documents folder.

- Desktop displays the Desktop.

- Favorites displays a list of the documents you've added to your Favorites list.

- Web Folders displays a list of web servers you can use to store a document.

3 Alternatively, use the Save In drop-down list box to select the drive holding the disk on which you want to save the document. Locate the folder in which you want to save the document in the large list box. Double-click the folder. (You might need to repeat this step to save a document in a subfolder within a folder.)

 To make backing up your important documents easier, save all the documents you create in the My Documents folder or in a subfolder within that folder. You can often use the Save As dialog box to create a subfolder by clicking the Create New Folder toolbar button.

4 Enter a name for the document in the File Name text box.

*Windows lets you name the document almost anything you choose. For example, if you want, you can create document names that are really, really long (up to 255 characters including spaces). Only a few characters are off limits in document names—for example, slashes, quotation marks, colons, asterisks, and question marks. However, I don't recommend using long document names because some other **operating systems** and programs can read only eight-letter names. So try to stick to short document names. If you do choose to use longer names, make sure that the first six letters clearly identify the document in case the long name gets truncated.*

 *You don't need to enter a **file extension** as part of a document name. The program adds the file extension for you.*

5 Click Save.

 Word 2000 saves documents in a format that is compatible with the previous version of Word, Word 97. This backward compatibility is notable because, unfortunately, it didn't exist between Word 97 and its predecessor.

Saving Documents as Web Pages

One of the biggest new features of Office 2000 is the convenient web-publishing capability. All of the Office programs allow you to publish web pages to a web server as easily as you save documents to your hard drive.

Setting Up Web Folders

To take full advantage of the ease of Office 2000's web-publishing capabilities, you need to set up web folders on the web server to which you intend to publish Office documents. If you want to publish documents to the **Internet,** you set up a web folder on your ISP's (Internet service provider's) web server. To publish documents on an internal **web site**, you set up a web folder on a web server on your local network.

To set up a web folder, follow these steps:

1 Choose the File Menu's Save As Web Page command, and click Web Folders on the Places bar.

2 Click the Create New Folder toolbar button. This starts the Add Web Folder Wizard, as shown in Figure 1-7.

FIGURE 1-7

The Add Web Folder Wizard.

3 Enter the **URL** (uniform resource locator) of the folder on the web server to which you want to publish. For example,
http://www.abccompany.com/documents

4 If the Add Web Folder Wizard prompts you for your user name and **password**, enter them in the boxes provided and click OK.

 If you don't know your web server's URL or your user name or password, contact your ISP or network administrator.

5 Click Finish.

Publishing an Office Document to a Web Folder

The web publishing features of each Office program vary slightly, but the basic process is the same. To publish an Office document to a web server, follow these steps:

1 Choose the File menu's Save As Web Page command.

2 Click Web Folders on the Places bar to display a list of the web folders you've set up, as shown in Figure 1-8.

FIGURE 1-8

Publishing a web page to a web folder using Word.

3 Open the web folder to which you want to publish by double-clicking it.

4 Click Change, and use the Set Page Title dialog box to enter a title for the web page. The title will be displayed in the **web browser** title bar when a person views the web page.

5 Enter a filename for the web page in the File Name text box.

Notes *Excel and PowerPoint have a few extra web publishing options. In Excel, for example, you can choose to publish only the active sheet or the entire workbook. Click Publish to set other publishing options, such as which items in the document you want to publish.*

6 Click Save.

Importing and Exporting Documents

If you want to work with an Office document using a non-Office or non-Windows program, you should export the document. Exporting a document means saving it in a format that the other program can easily read. If you want to work with a non-Office document in Office, you need to import the document. Importing a document means converting it from another format. By importing a document, you can, for example, take a **table** you created in an accounting program and work with it in Excel.

*The need to import and export commonly arises when you want to share information with people who use operating systems or programs different from yours. For example, you might want to share a document with someone using a Macintosh or a **word processor** such as Corel WordPerfect.*

Exporting Office Documents

To export an Office document so it can be used by a non-Office program, follow these steps:

1 Open the document you want to export in the Office program you used to create the document.

2 Choose the File menu's Save As command to display a dialog box similar to the one shown in Figure 1-9.

FIGURE 1-9

The Save As dialog box in Word.

3 Use the Save As Type drop-down list box to specify how you want to save the document. For example, if you want to save a document so you can open it and work with it on a Macintosh, save the document in a Macintosh format.

 Different programs have different document types available.

4 Optionally, specify a new location for storing the document. Use the Save In drop-down list box to select the drive, such as your floppy drive, on which you want to save the document. Locate the folder in which you want to save the document in the large list box. Once you find the folder, double-click it.

 Notes *If this is the first time you're saving the document, you need to also specify a document name using the File Name text box.*

5 Click Save.

6 Open the document using the other program.

Importing Documents into Office

To work with a non-Office document using an Office program, follow these steps:

1 Export the document from its source program, if that has not already been done.

 Some programs have a special command on the File menu specifically for exporting, instead of the Save As command. Usually, this command is named something like Export.

---

2 Open the Office program in which you want to work with the document.

3 Choose the File menu's Open command to display a dialog box similar to the one shown in Figure 1-10. Use this dialog box to locate the document you want to import.

FIGURE 1-10

The Open dialog box in Excel.

4 Use the Files Of Type drop-down list box to specify the type of document you're looking for.

5 Select the document, and click Open. The program might start a wizard to help you convert the document format.

Closing Documents

After you finish working with a document and save your changes, you close the document. Most Office programs don't require you to close one document before opening another, but some do. Even if a program doesn't require you to close a document, it's a good practice to do so. Closing the documents you're not using cleans up your workspace and frees up computer resources so your computer runs more efficiently.

To keep your document changes, make sure you save the document before you close it.

You have two ways to close a document. Either way, you must first display the document you want to close. Then, you can either click the **document window's** Close button (located in the upper right corner with an X on it) or choose the File menu's Close command.

 If you're working with an Office program that lets you open more than one document at a time, you can choose the File menu's Close All command to close all the open documents simultaneously. Note, however, that the Close All command doesn't appear on the File menu unless you press the Shift key before you open the menu.

Exiting Office Programs

When you're finished using a program and have saved all the documents you were working on within that program, you're ready to exit. You should always exit any programs you don't plan to use for a while. This enables your computer to do the tasks you are working on faster.

As with closing documents, you have two ways to exit a program. You can either click the program's Close button or choose the File menu's Exit command.

 If you can't close an Office program by clicking its Close button or choosing its Exit command, you may need to tell Windows to close the program. To do this, press the Ctrl, Alt, and Del keys simultaneously. Windows then displays the Close Program dialog box, which lists all the programs you're running. To close the unresponsive Office program, click it to select it from the list, and then click End Task.

Getting Help Within Office

When you're stumped trying to figure out how to do something in Office, help is generally only a click away. All of the Office programs provide both an **Office Assistant** and extensive online help.

*Some dialog boxes in Office (as in other Windows programs) contain a question-mark button next to the Close button. Click the question-mark button and then click an option in the dialog box to display an explanation of the option in a **pop-up window**. Click outside the pop-up window to close it. You can also right-click an option to display What's This?*

Using the Office Assistant

The Office Assistant is the little cartoon character you see moving about in an Office program's window. If you don't see the Office Assistant, you can tell the program to start the Office Assistant by choosing the Help menu's Show The Office Assistant command.

To ask the Office Assistant a question, click the Office Assistant. When you do this, the Office Assistant displays the What Would You Like To Do? bubble. Type your question in the box, and click Search. The Office Assistant displays a list of help topics in answer to your question, as shown in Figure 1-11. To read a help topic, click it. When you do, the Office Assistant displays the help topic in its own window, as shown in Figure 1-12.

FIGURE 1-11

The Office Assistant.

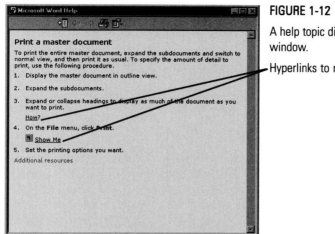

FIGURE 1-12

A help topic displayed in its own window.

Hyperlinks to related articles.

Help articles often include **hyperlinks** at the bottom of the article, which link to other related articles. When you're using Help, you might also see terms in color. If you don't know what one of these terms means, click it to display an explanation in a pop-up window, as shown in Figure 1-13.

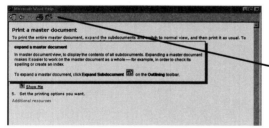

FIGURE 1-13

Word Help explains *Expand* in a pop-up window.

The Help toolbar.

The toolbar at the top of the window has Back and Forward buttons you use to navigate within the Help program in the same way that the Internet Explorer's Back and Forward buttons let you navigate the **World Wide Web.** To retrace your path through Help, click the Back toolbar button; to then go back to where you were, click the Forward toolbar button.

Notes *Chapter 8 describes how to work with Internet Explorer and navigate the World Wide Web.*

In addition, the toolbar includes the following buttons:

- Show shows Help's tabs. Click the Show toolbar button again to hide the tabs.
- Print prints the currently displayed help topic.
- Options contains a menu of commands for working with Help.

If the Office Assistant doesn't provide the answer you're looking for, you can browse through help topics on your own. To do so, click the Show toolbar button in the Help window to show Help's tabs (see Figure 1-14).

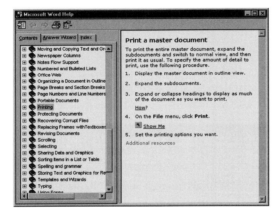

FIGURE 1-14

The Help window with tabs displayed.

Using the Contents Tab

To use the Contents tab, click the tab and then click a topic's book icon to display the topic's subtopics. If necessary, click a subtopic's book icon to display still more subtopics. Then click an article heading to open a description and instructions for this topic in the right pane of the window. For example, to open instructions on how to preview a document before printing, as shown in Figure 1-15, follow these steps:

1 Click the Printing book icon.

2 Click Preview A Document Before Printing to display the article shown in Figure 1-15.

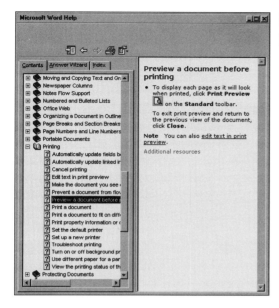

FIGURE 1-15

Help on previewing a document.

Using the Answer Wizard Tab

The Contents tab is one way of finding information in Office Help, but using one of Help's search engines, such as the Answer Wizard or Index tab, often produces quicker, more accurate results. When you use the Answer Wizard tab, as shown in Figure 1-16, Help looks through the actual contents of help topics and displays a list of all those that contain your search term or phrase.

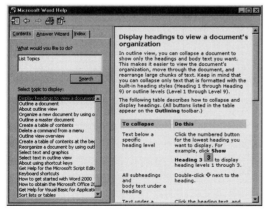

FIGURE 1-16

The Answer Wizard tab.

Let's enter a question and see what the Answer Wizard comes up with. To see how this works, follow these steps:

1   Click the Answer Wizard tab, if necessary.

2   In the What Would You Like To Do? text box, enter *How do I create a Table of Contents?*

3   Click Search. Office Help displays a list of topics, as shown in Figure 1-17.

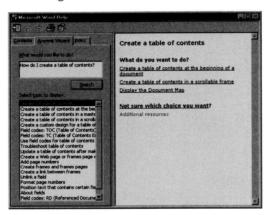

FIGURE 1-17

The Answer Wizard's results for how to create a table of contents.

4   Select the topic you want to read about from the Select Topic To Display list.

 Some topics contain links to a wizard that will walk you through the steps involved in doing something. To access the wizard, click the Click Here hyperlink in the topic.

Using the Index Tab

When you click the Index tab, Help takes you through a three-step process in narrowing your search and finding the correct Help article. Let's try to find an article on **databases.** To see how this works, follow these steps:

1   Click the Index tab, if necessary.

2   Enter the word *database* in the Type Keywords text box, and click Search. Help displays a list of topics in the Or Choose Keywords list box. If the exact topic you enter is not displayed, select a related topic in the Or Choose Keywords box by clicking it.

3 Select a topic from the Choose A Topic list box. Help displays the topic in the right frame, as shown in Figure 1-18.

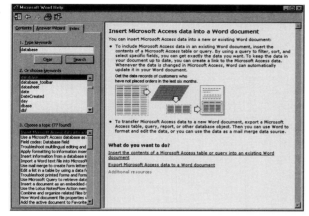

FIGURE 1-18

The Index tab.

CHAPTER 2

Common Office Tasks

2

One of the most valuable aspects of Microsoft Office 2000 is that once you know how to take care of essential tasks in one **program**, you can apply those skills to all the other programs. For example, if you know how to enter information in a **Microsoft Excel 2000** worksheet, you also know how to enter information in a **Microsoft Access 2000** *table.* And if you know how to print a **Microsoft Word 2000** *document,* you also know how to print **Microsoft PowerPoint 2000** *slides.*

In this chapter, we're going to take a look at the features common to all Office programs. Regardless of the program you're using, you do the following tasks in basically the same way:

- Entering and editing text
- Using the **Personal toolbar**
- Using the Office drawing tools
- Printing documents
- Inserting **objects** in a document
- Working with **hyperlinks**

Entering and Editing Text

The first thing you need to know about entering and editing text is that you do so at the **insertion point**. The insertion point, shown in Figure 2-1, is the flashing vertical bar you see as soon as you open a document. The only exception is Excel. Excel displays the insertion point after you type the first character.

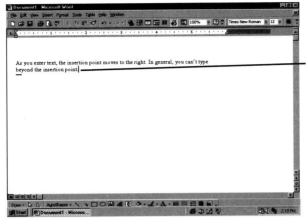

Entering Text

In general, you can't enter text beyond the insertion point. However, a new feature in Word 2000, **Click-and-Type**, allows you to enter text almost anywhere in your document at any time. Simply **double-click** where you want to enter text, and start typing. You can also use Click-and-Type to insert an object, a process discussed in the later section "Inserting Objects in a Document."

 *You must be in Web Layout or Print Layout **view** to use Click-and-Type.*

You can't enter much text in an Office program without discovering a feature called **AutoCorrect.** To see what I'm talking about, open a program, type *teh* at the insertion point, and press the Spacebar. Instantly, you'll see *teh* become *the.* And, just for fun, type *:)* and press the Spacebar to see a graphical smiley face replace the keyboard characters.

 *AutoCorrect is not available in **Microsoft Outlook 2000**. It is available in the other Office programs.*

You can use AutoCorrect to do much more, however, than correcting the spelling of *the* or automatically inserting a graphical smiley face. To take a look at your options, choose the Tools **menu's** AutoCorrect command to display the AutoCorrect **dialog box**, as shown in Figure 2-2.

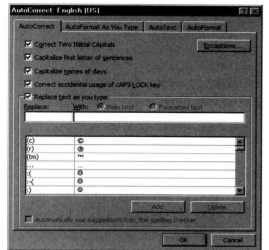

FIGURE 2-2

Use the vertical scrollbar to scan
the list of corrections that come
with Office.

By default, all the options in the upper part of the AutoCorrect dialog
box are checked. If the work you do involves regular use of some word
or term that violates one of these rules, clear the check box. To add a
term to the list in the lower part of the AutoCorrect dialog box, type its
common misspelling in the Replace text box and its correct spelling in
the With text box. To customize the rules that AutoCorrect follows, **click**
Exceptions and establish your own rules using the AutoCorrect Exceptions dialog box.

Editing Text

Of course, AutoCorrect doesn't do all your editing for you. Your two
most frequently used tools are likely to be the Backspace key and the
Delete key. Just remember: pressing Backspace deletes the character to
the *left* of the insertion point; pressing Delete deletes the character to the
right of the insertion point.

Vying closely for most-used status in the editing process are the Undo
and Redo buttons on the Personal toolbar, as shown in Figure 2-3. This
toolbar is discussed in the later section "Using the Personal Toolbar,"
but let's discuss these buttons here.

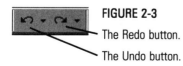

FIGURE 2-3

The Redo button.

The Undo button.

In Figure 2-3, the button on the left is the Undo button. Clicking Undo essentially reverses an action you have just taken, a series of actions, or any action that is on the history list, as shown in Figure 2-4. To display the history, click the Down arrow button next to the Undo button.

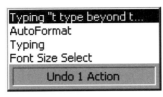

FIGURE 2-4

To reverse an action on the history list, simply click it.

If you click the Undo button and change your mind, simply click Redo.

You should also be aware of the two editing modes in Office: Insert and Overtype. In Insert mode, entering new text simply moves existing text to the right. In Overtype mode, entering new text replaces existing text. The default is Insert mode. If you want to use Overtype mode, press the Insert key. To get back to Insert mode, press the Insert key again.

Copying Text

You can **copy** text from one place in your document to another place in your document, and you can copy text from one Office program to another Office program. Before you do either, however, you have to select text. Although each program has its own shortcuts for selecting, you can always **drag** to select text. Simply click where you want to start defining a selection, hold down the mouse button, drag to where you want to end the selection, and release the mouse button. Your selection appears in reverse video; that is, the text is light, and the background is dark. To unselect text, click outside the area you selected.

 After you select text, pressing any key on the keyboard deletes the selection. If you accidentally delete some text, simply click the Undo toolbar button.

When you copy text, the original remains exactly as it was when you selected it, and a copy is placed on the **Clipboard.** The Clipboard is an area in the computer's memory that Microsoft Windows uses as a temporary storage container. To copy text, follow these steps:

1 Select the text, and choose the File menu's Copy command or click the Copy toolbar button.

2 Place the insertion point where you want the copy.

3 Choose the File menu's Paste command, or click the Paste toolbar button.

 Notes *Instead of using the menu commands or toolbar buttons, you can press Ctrl+C to copy a selection, and then press Ctrl+V to **paste** it.*

Moving Text

To move text, follow these steps:

1 Select the text, and choose the File menu's Cut command.

2 Place the insertion point where you want to move the selection.

3 Choose the File menu's Paste command.

 Notes *Instead of using the File menu's Cut command, you can press Ctrl+X.*

Collecting and Pasting

In Office 2000, you can copy as many as 12 items to the Clipboard, even items from several programs, and then paste them in another document or another program. To do this, you use the Clipboard toolbar, as shown in Figure 2-5.

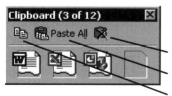

FIGURE 2-5

The Clipboard toolbar.

The Clear Clipboard button.

The Paste All button.

The Copy button.

To display the Clipboard toolbar, choose the View menu's Toolbars command and then choose the submenu's Clipboard command. To copy multiple items and then paste them using the Clipboard toolbar, follow these steps:

1 Select the text to copy, and click the Copy button. Do this for as many items (up to 12) as you want to copy.

2 Place the insertion point where you want the items (perhaps in another document or another program), display the Clipboard toolbar (if necessary), and click the Paste All button.

Office automatically keeps the last 12 items you copy or **cut** on the Clipboard. To clear the Clipboard, click the Clear Clipboard button.

Using the Personal Toolbar

The Personal toolbar, shown in Figure 2-6, is a new feature in Office 2000, and by default it contains some of the buttons that were formerly on the Standard and Formatting toolbars in one row. As you use menu commands and toolbar buttons, Office replaces the default buttons and commands with those you use most often.

FIGURE 2-6

The Personal toolbar in Excel.

To see a button's name, simply point to it. Office displays a ScreenTip showing the button's name and its associated shortcut keys. If you prefer, you can reset the Personal toolbar so that your screen displays the Standard and Formatting toolbars on two rows. To do this, follow these steps:

1 Choose the Tools menu's Customize command to display the Customize dialog box, as shown in Figure 2-7.

2 Click the Options tab.

3 Clear the Standard And Formatting Toolbars Share One Row check box.

4 Click Close.

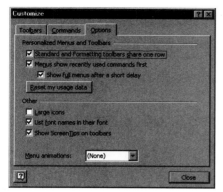

FIGURE 2-7

The Customize dialog box.

If at any time you want to return the toolbar to its default state, click Reset My Usage Data on the Options tab in the Customize dialog box.

Table 2-1 lists the buttons on the default Personal toolbar that are common to all Office programs and describes what each does.

Button	What It Does
Open	Opens an existing document.
Save	Saves the open document.
Print	Prints the open document.
Print Preview	Displays on-screen what the open document will look like printed.
Cut	Moves the selection from the document to the Clipboard.
Copy	Copies the selection to the Clipboard.
Paste	Copies the selection on the Clipboard to the location specified by the insertion point.
Undo	Reverses an action.
Redo	Reverses a previous Undo action.
Zoom	Increases or decreases the size of the display.
Help	Opens the Help files for the running program.
Font	Lets you select a typeface from a drop-down list.
Size	Lets you select a **font** size.

TABLE 2-1: The buttons common to all Office programs that are available on the Personal toolbar.

To see a list of all the tools available on a toolbar, click the More Buttons button (the one with the **double chevron**). To manually add or remove buttons, click the Add Or Remove Buttons button. Then check a button to add it, or clear a button's check box to remove it.

Each Office program provides a number of other toolbars. You can display a list of these other toolbars by choosing the View menu's Toolbars command. Some programs display certain toolbars automatically when you start a related task. For example, when you insert a chart, the Office program displays the Chart toolbar. In Excel and PowerPoint, the Drawing toolbar is displayed at the bottom of your screen when you open the program, and the Drawing toolbar is also available in Word.

Using the Office Drawing Tools

You use the tools on the Drawing toolbar to create your own graphics. To display the Drawing toolbar, choose the View menu's Toolbars command and click Drawing, or click the Drawing button if it is available on the Personal toolbar. Figure 2-8 shows the Drawing toolbar. Point to a button to display its name in a ScreenTip. Table 2-2 lists the buttons on the Drawing toolbar and describes what each does.

 You can also right-click any toolbar and choose the shortcut menu's Drawing command to display the Drawing toolbar.

 The Drawing toolbar is not available in Access, but you can create a drawing in another program and paste it into an Access database.

FIGURE 2-8

The Drawing toolbar.

Button	What It Does
Draw	Displays a menu from which you can choose commands that arrange drawn objects.
Select Objects	Allows you to select several drawn objects at once.
Free Rotate	Allows you to rotate a drawn object.
AutoShapes	Displays a menu of drawn objects that you can insert in a document.
Line	Draws a straight line.
Arrow	Draws an arrow.
Rectangle	Draws a rectangle. Hold down the Shift key and drag to draw a square.
Oval	Draws an oval. Hold down the Shift key and drag to draw a circle.
Text Box	Draws a **text box**.
Insert WordArt	Starts the **WordArt** program.
Insert Clip Art	Opens the Microsoft Clip Art Gallery, from which you can choose images to insert in your document.
Fill Color	Opens a palette of colors that you can use to choose a fill color for the selected object.
Line Color	Opens a palette of colors that you can use to color a selected line.
Font Color	Opens a palette of colors that you can use to color selected text.
Line Style	Opens a list of line styles in various widths that you can apply to a selected line.
Dash Style	Opens a list of dashed line styles that you can apply to a selected line.
Arrow Style	Opens a list of arrow styles that you can apply to a selected arrow.
Shadow	Displays a selection of shadows that you can apply to a selected drawn object.
3-D	Displays a selection of 3-D effects that you can apply to a selected drawn object.

TABLE 2-2: The buttons on the Drawing toolbar (from left to right).

You use the buttons on the left half of the Drawing toolbar to create objects, and you use the buttons on the right half to format existing drawn objects. Figure 2-9 shows some simple graphics that were created using the tools on the Drawing toolbar.

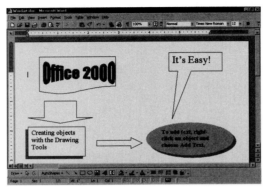

FIGURE 2-9

You can create simple objects such as these or objects that are much more complicated using the tools on the Drawing toolbar.

Now let's look in more detail at how to use some of the individual Drawing tools, starting with AutoShapes. Clicking the AutoShapes button opens a list of AutoShape categories, as shown in Figure 2-10.

FIGURE 2-10

Click a category to display graphic examples.

To insert an AutoShape, simply click it and then drag to insert it in your document. If you're adding lots of shapes (perhaps you're creating a flow chart), you can click the top of the menu and drag it onto your document. To add text to any AutoShape, select it, right-click its edge, and choose the shortcut menu's Add Text command. You can then add the text and format it using all the usual formatting tools and menus.

To insert line art objects, you select the tool—Line, Arrow, Rectangle, or Oval—click in your document, and drag to draw the object. After you draw the object, you can select it and drag any of its handles (the little squares that appear around it) to resize it. To move it, click the object and drag.

When you're drawing an arrow, the arrowhead appears at the end of the line when you release the mouse button. When you're drawing rectangles or squares, drag from one corner of the object diagonally to the opposite corner. When drawing ovals or circles, use the same technique, imagining an invisible rectangle framing the oval or circle.

The Insert WordArt button is in the middle of the toolbar, and clicking it allows you to create a WordArt image. You can use WordArt to create logos, emphasize titles, and add some pizzazz to a document. To do so, follow these steps:

1 Click the Insert WordArt button to display the WordArt Gallery, as shown in Figure 2-11.

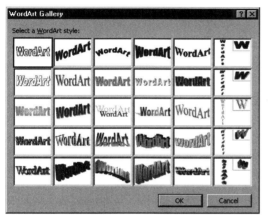

FIGURE 2-11

The WordArt Gallery.

2 Select a style, and click OK to display the Edit WordArt Text dialog box, as shown in Figure 2-12.

FIGURE 2-12

Replace "Your Text Here" with your text.

3 Type your text, and use the buttons at the top of the dialog box to format it.

4 Click OK to insert the WordArt object in your document and open the WordArt toolbar, as shown in Figure 2-13.

FIGURE 2-13

Use the buttons on the WordArt toolbar to format and enhance your WordArt object.

You can now use the WordArt toolbar to edit your text, rotate it, wrap text around it, align it with other objects, space out the characters, and so on. Point to a tool to see its name in a ScreenTip. Table 2-3 lists the buttons on the WordArt toolbar and describes what each does. As usual, to move a WordArt object, simply select it and then drag it.

Button	What It Does
Insert WordArt	Opens the WordArt Gallery so you can create a new WordArt object.
Edit Text	Opens the Edit WordArt Text dialog box so you can change the text.
WordArt Gallery	Opens the WordArt Gallery so you can change the WordArt style.
Format WordArt	Opens the Format WordArt dialog box so you can format colors and lines, size, and layout elements, and enter some alternative text if you are creating a **web page**.
WordArt Shape	Opens a menu of shapes that you can select and then pour the text into.
Free Rotate	Changes the object handles to rotation handles so you can rotate the text, that is, turn it on its side or upside down. Click the Free Rotate button again to turn it off.
Text Wrapping	Opens a menu of various ways you can wrap text around your WordArt object.
WordArt Same Letter Heights	Makes all the letters the same height, regardless of case.
WordArt Vertical Text	Changes the orientation of the object to vertical rather than horizontal. To change it back, click the WordArt Vertical Text button again.

Button	What It Does
WordArt Alignment	Opens a menu you can use to align the object: Left Align, Center, Right Align, Word Justify, Letter Justify, and Stretch Justify.
WordArt Character Spacing	Opens a menu you can use to adjust the spacing between letters: Very Tight, Tight, Normal, Loose, Very Loose, and Custom. This menu also contains a Kern Character Pairs command.

TABLE 2-3: The buttons on the WordArt toolbar (from left to right).

As mentioned earlier, after you draw an object, you can format it using the buttons on the right half of the Drawing toolbar. Let's quickly take a look at them. To apply the styles associated with these buttons, you always first select the object and then click the button.

As an example, let's say you've drawn a square in your document. Now you can do the following:

- To color the square, click the Fill Color button and select a color.

- To color the lines that outline the square, click the Line Color button and select a color.

- To insert text in your square, right-click it and choose Add Text from the shortcut menu.

- To color the text you just added, select it, click the Font Color button, and select a color.

- To make the outline lines thicker, click the Line Style button and select a style.

- To change the solid outline lines to dashed lines, click the Dash Style button and select a dashed line style.

- To place a shadow around your square, click the Shadow button and select a shadow type.

- To add a 3-D enhancement, click the 3-D button and select a style.

You may not have created a work of art in the tradition of Van Gogh or Picasso, but now you know how to format the Drawing objects you insert in your documents.

The Draw menu, the first item on the Drawing toolbar, contains a number of options you can use to manipulate objects. When you add several objects to a document, the Office program places them in separate layers, and you can move objects from layer to layer. As usual, before you select an option, be sure to select the object you want to manipulate. So that you see how this works, draw a rectangle in your document, and then draw an oval that partially covers the rectangle, as shown in Figure 2-14.

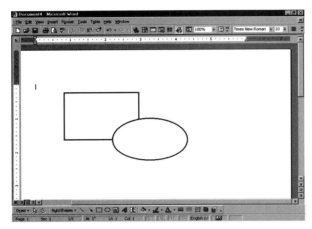

FIGURE 2-14

Play with these simple graphics to get a feel for how the Draw menu works.

- To send the oval behind the rectangle, choose the Draw menu's Order command, and then choose the submenu's Send To Back command.

- To move the oval back in front of the rectangle, choose the Draw menu's Order command, and then choose either Send To Front or Bring Forward.

Now, right-click the circle, and choose the shortcut menu's Add Text command. Add some text, and select the rectangle. Choose the Draw menu's Order command, and then choose the submenu's Bring In Front Of Text command. You'll see that the square now partially covers the text. To display the text again, choose the Draw menu's Order command, and then choose the submenu's Send Behind Text command.

When your drawing is complete, you might want to group all the drawing objects so you can treat them as a single object. For example, you might want to do this if you plan to insert the drawing in another document or in another program. To group multiple objects, select all the objects and choose the Draw menu's Group command. The handles on the selected objects are replaced with one set of handles that you can use to size or move the entire object, as shown in Figure 2-15. To ungroup an object, simply select it and then choose the Draw menu's Ungroup command.

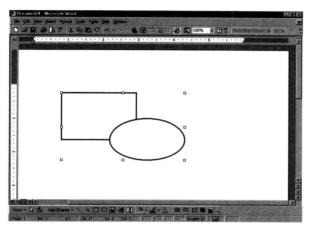

FIGURE 2-15

Now the two drawings form one object.

 To select multiple objects, hold down the Shift key and then click each object.

Printing Documents

The easiest way to print a document in any Office program is to click the Print button on the Personal toolbar. Behind the scenes the Office program creates a spool **file** (a printable copy of the document) and sends it to Windows. Then, Windows actually prints the document.

Clicking the Print toolbar button prints the entire active document using the printer you last specified (or using your default printer if you haven't specified a different printer since starting the Office program). For example, if you're working on a 100-page report in Word, clicking the Print button prints all 100 pages. If you're working on a PowerPoint **presentation**, clicking the Print button prints the entire presentation in Slide **view.** If this is what you want, fine. But most of the time, you'll want more control over what's printed and how it looks on the page.

Setting Up the Pages of a Printed Document

To tell an Office program how you want your document to appear on the printed page, you use the Page Setup dialog box. The options available in this dialog box depend on the program, but in most Office programs you specify margins, paper size, **page orientation**, paper source, and so forth. To display the Page Setup dialog box, choose the File menu's Page Setup command. Figure 2-16 shows the Page Setup dialog box in Access, and Figure 2-17 shows the Page Setup dialog box in Word.

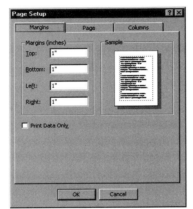

FIGURE 2-16

The Margins tab in Access's Page Setup dialog box.

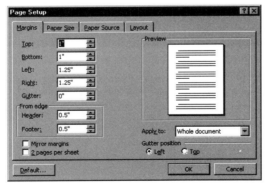

FIGURE 2-17

The Margins tab in Word's Page Setup dialog box.

This section describes how you set up the elements that are common in most Office programs and illustrates the process using Word's Page Setup dialog box.

When you're setting up pages in any Page Setup dialog box, you can always click the Help button (the one with the question mark) and then click anything in the dialog box to display a ScreenTip that explains the option.

You use the Margins tab to specify the print area of the page. By default, Word starts the print area 1 inch from the top edge of the page and stops at 1 inch from the bottom. The left and right margins are set at 1.25 inches. To change any of these settings, click the up and down arrows until you see the setting you want, or select the measurement and enter a new setting. If your document has headers and footers, you can accept Word's default specifications or change them, just as you change the other margins.

You specify paper size and page orientation using the Paper Size tab, as shown in Figure 2-18.

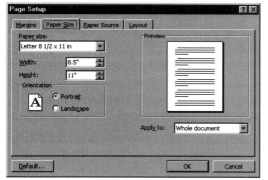

FIGURE 2-18

The Paper Size tab in Word's Page Setup dialog box.

If you want to print on paper that's not 8½ by 11 inches in size, select a different size from the Paper Size drop-down list box. You'll see the dimensions change in the Width and Height boxes. To specify a custom-size sheet of paper, enter the dimensions directly in the Width and Height boxes.

Orientation refers to the direction of the paper. Portrait prints vertically; that is, the 8½-inch side of the paper is the top of the page. Landscape prints horizontally; that is, the 11-inch side of the paper is the top of the page. Most of the time in Word, you'll probably use the Portrait orientation; and most of the time in Excel, you'll probably want to print in Landscape orientation. By default, PowerPoint prints slides in Landscape orientation.

Click the Paper Source tab to specify the paper tray your printer will use. The options in the drop-down lists reflect the paper feed options available on your current printer.

 In Excel, you specify paper size, orientation, and paper source by clicking Options in the Page Setup dialog box and then clicking the Paper tab. In PowerPoint, click Properties in the Print dialog box to access the Paper tab.

Previewing a To-Be-Printed Document

The Print Preview feature is available in all Office programs except PowerPoint, and using it saves trees, printer cartridges, and time. To see exactly how your pages will look when printed, click the Print Preview toolbar button or choose the File menu's Print Preview command. In some programs, you can also click Print Preview in the Page Setup dialog box. Figure 2-19 shows an Excel worksheet in Print Preview, and Figure 2-20 shows a Word document in Print Preview.

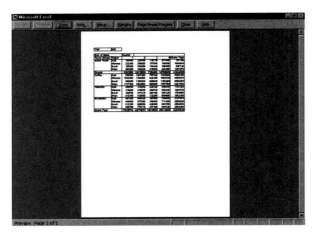

FIGURE 2-19

An Excel worksheet in Print Preview.

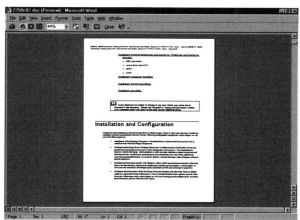

FIGURE 2-20

A Word document in Print Preview.

As you can see, the options available in Print Preview depend on the program. In all programs that have Print Preview, however, you can print, zoom, close, and get help. In Word, you can actually edit the document in Print Preview as well as adjust the page setup settings. In the other programs, you can't edit but you can adjust the page setup settings.

To page back and forth through your preview document, press the Page Up and Page Down keys. To zoom in and out of the document, click it.

Printing a Document

When you're finally ready to print your document, you can do so in several ways. As mentioned earlier, the easiest way is to click the Print toolbar button. Clicking the Print toolbar button prints the entire active document, using the default settings in the Page Setup dialog box or those you've established. For more control over what's printed, however, you'll want to use the Print dialog box. You can open this dialog box by clicking the Print toolbar button in Print Preview or by choosing the File menu's Print command. Figure 2-21 shows Word's Print dialog box.

The options in the Print dialog box depend on the program, but all Print dialog boxes work in much the same way as Word's Print dialog box.

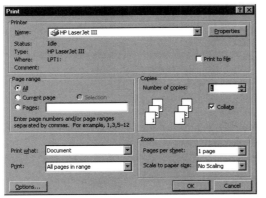

FIGURE 2-21

Word's Print dialog box.

You use the Print dialog box primarily to tell a program what to print on which printer. If your computer is connected to more than one printer, you select the one to print to from the Name drop-down list box. The lower part of the Printer section of this dialog box displays the printer's status. You can click Properties to display the Properties dialog box for the selected printer. Figure 2-22 shows this dialog box, which is the same dialog box you display in Excel when you click Options in the Page Setup dialog box.

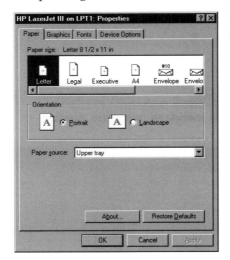

FIGURE 2-22

The Printer Properties dialog box.

Notes *Different printers have radically different Printer Properties dialog boxes, so don't worry if yours looks different from the one shown in Figure 2-22.*

If you want to change the paper size, page orientation, or paper source, you can do so in this Properties box instead of the Page Setup dialog box. If you make changes, click OK to return to the Print dialog box.

From the options under Page Range in the Print dialog box, specify whether you want to print the entire document, the current page, a selection, or only certain pages. From the options under Copies, indicate the number of copies of each page that you want, and then select the Collate check box if you want all pages printed successively. If you don't select this check box and you specify, for example, three copies, then three copies of page 1 are printed, three copies of page 2 are printed, and so on. You'll end up doing the work of the Collate function.

To see what else you can print besides the active document, click the arrow in the Print What drop-down list box. Table 2-4 lists what you can print in Excel, PowerPoint, and Word.

Office Program	What You Can Print
Excel	A selection, an entire **workbook,** the active sheet.
PowerPoint	Slides, handouts, notes pages, Outline view.
Word	The document, document properties, comments, **styles, AutoText** entries, key assignments.

TABLE 2-4: What you can print.

In the Print drop-down list box, you can choose to print all pages in a range or only odd or only even pages. Use the odd/even options when you're printing on both sides of the paper.

If you start printing a document and change your mind, follow these steps to cancel the print job:

1 Minimize the program, click the Start button, choose Settings, and click Printers to display the Printers dialog box, as shown in Figure 2-23.

FIGURE 2-23

Use the Printers dialog box to cancel a print job.

2 Double-click the icon for your printer to display its dialog box.

3 Select the name of the document for which you want to cancel printing.

4 Choose the Document menu's Cancel Printing command.

In the Print dialog box of all Office programs, you'll notice a Print To File check box. Printing to a file is saving a copy of a document file in a file format that a printer can read rather than sending the file to the printer. You may seldom or never need this option, but it's useful if you ever want to print a document file later, on a different computer or printer, or if you want to use the file in a desktop publishing program. To print to a file, follow these steps:

1 In the Print dialog box, select the Print To File check box and click OK to display the Print To File dialog box, as shown in Figure 2-24.

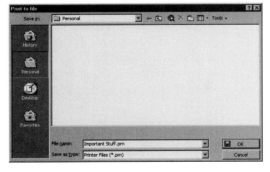

FIGURE 2-24

The Print To File dialog box.

2 Enter a name for the file in the File Name text box. The file will automatically be given the .prn extension that printer files use.

3 Select the **folder** in which you want to save the file.

4 Click OK.

Inserting Objects in a Document

In Office 2000, the term *object* applies to many things—tables, charts, video clips, pictures, graphics you create with the Draw program, sound clips, an Excel worksheet, a PowerPoint presentation, an Access database, and so on. You can insert almost any type of object in any Office program, but each program gives you menu or toolbar access to the types of objects you're most likely to use in that program.

To insert an object in an Office program, start with the Insert menu. Choose the command for the type of object you want to insert. For example, you might want to insert a picture in a Word document. So choose the Insert menu's Picture command, and then from the submenu, select the kind of picture—clip art, a photo you've saved in a file, an AutoShape, a WordArt graphic, a file from a scanner or a digital camera, or a chart. In Excel, in addition to most of these types of objects, you'll find an organization chart on the Picture submenu. In PowerPoint, the Picture submenu contains most of the items on the Excel Picture submenu, plus the Microsoft Word Table command.

Notes   *Chapter 3 describes how to insert pictures in a document.*

If the Insert menu doesn't list the type of object you want to insert, choose the Insert menu's Object command to display the Object dialog box. If you want to insert an existing file, select the Create From File tab, as shown in Figure 2-25. Enter the name of the file in the File Name text box, or click Browse to locate it. Click OK to insert the file in your document.

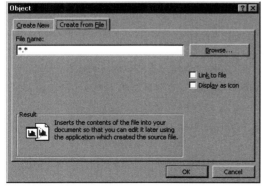

FIGURE 2-25

The Create From File tab in the Object dialog box.

Before you insert any object, place the insertion point where you want the file inserted.

If you want to create a new file to insert as an object, click the Create New tab, as shown in Figure 2-26. The Object Type list includes the programs installed on your computer. Selecting one of these programs opens it within the current document. For example, if you want to insert a new Excel worksheet in a Word document, select Microsoft Excel Worksheet from the Object Type list and click OK. Word displays an Excel worksheet in your document, and the Excel Personal toolbar at the top of the **document window,** as shown in Figure 2-27. You can now enter data for your worksheet just as you would if you opened Excel from the Start menu. Once you insert an object, you can move and resize it using the selection handles.

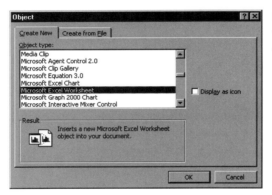

FIGURE 2-26

The Create New tab in the Object dialog box.

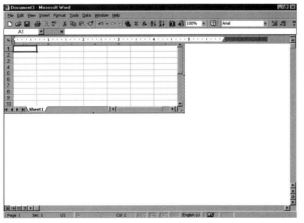

FIGURE 2-27

An empty Excel worksheet open in a Word document, ready for your data.

Notes As you install new programs on your computer, the Office program adds their names to the Object Type list. But the Object Type list may also include programs that you have removed from your computer. If you try to insert one of these objects, you get an error message.

Even if you don't select the Display As Icon check box, Office programs insert some objects as icons. For example, if you insert a sound file, the Office program displays it as an icon. Double-click the icon to play the sound.

2

Working with Hyperlinks

A hyperlink is colored and underlined text or a graphic that, when clicked, opens a resource. This resource could be almost anything—a file on your hard drive, a site on the **Internet**, a sound or movie clip, a chat room, and so on. To check this out and to see how easy it is to insert and use a hyperlink, follow these steps:

1 Open an Office program, and click where you want to place a hyperlink.

2 Choose the Insert menu's Hyperlink command to display the Insert Hyperlink dialog box.

3 In the Type The File Or Web Page Name text box, enter the name of a file on your hard drive, or click File, and select a file.

4 Click OK in the Link To File dialog box, and then click OK again in the Insert Hyperlink dialog box.

5 The Office program inserts the name of the file at the insertion point. Click the hyperlinked filename to open the file in the program used to create the file.

If the file to which you created a link also includes a link, you can click that link to open yet another resource.

The hyperlink we just created and inserted works, but it's not particularly attractive, and until you click it, you have no idea what it is or why you might want to open the resource to which it refers. Let's take a look at the Office tools you can use to create informative, inviting hyperlinks.

Inserting Hyperlinks in a Document

The easiest way to insert a hyperlink in an Office document is simply to type an **e-mail** address or a **URL** (uniform resource locator) directly in a document. The Office program immediately knows that it is a hyperlink and formats it as such. But by using the Insert Hyperlink dialog box you can create a significantly more useful hyperlink. To do so, follow these steps:

1   Place the insertion point where you want the hyperlink in your document, or select the text or graphic that you want to display for the hyperlink.

2   Choose the Insert menu's Hyperlink command or click the Insert Hyperlink toolbar button to display the Insert Hyperlink dialog box, as shown in Figure 2-28.

FIGURE 2-28

The Insert Hyperlink dialog box.

3   If you selected text, it is displayed in the Text To Display text box. If you did not select text, type the text that you want to appear in color and underlined.

4   In the Type The File Or Web Page Name text box, enter the filename or URL to which you want to link. Or select a resource from the list. If you don't see it in the list and don't know it, click File to locate it.

5   To attach a ScreenTip to the hyperlink, click ScreenTip to display the Set Hyperlink ScreenTip dialog box, as shown in Figure 2-29. A ScreenTip is text that appears in a little box when you rest the mouse pointer over a hyperlink. You can use it to supply more information about the resource to which you are linking.

FIGURE 2-29

The Set Hyperlink ScreenTip
dialog box.

6 In the ScreenTip Text box, enter the text you want to display, and then click OK.

7 Click OK once more in the Insert Hyperlink dialog box.

To insert an e-mail address as a hyperlink, you follow these same basic steps, but in the Insert Hyperlink dialog box, click the E-Mail Address shortcut. The Insert Hyperlink dialog box now looks like Figure 2-30.

FIGURE 2-30

Inserting an e-mail address
as a hyperlink.

Enter the text to display, enter the e-mail address, add a subject line if you want, create a ScreenTip if you want, and click OK. Clicking an e-mail hyperlink opens a message window in the user's default e-mail program; the To line is already filled in with the address associated with the hyperlink, and if you include a subject line, that is also filled in.

Editing a Hyperlink

You might want to edit a hyperlink for any number of reasons—the URL is no longer valid, the name of the file has changed, an e-mail address is no longer active, and so on. To edit a hyperlink, follow these steps:

1 Right-click the hyperlink, choose the shortcut menu's Hyperlink command, and choose the submenu's Edit Hyperlink command to display the Edit Hyperlink dialog box, as shown in Figure 2-31.

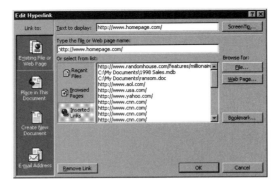

FIGURE 2-31

The Edit Hyperlink dialog box.

2   Now simply follow the steps in the previous section for inserting a hyperlink to change a filename, URL, or e-mail address, or to rewrite a ScreenTip, and so on.

Deleting a Hyperlink

You can't delete a hyperlink the way you normally delete text or a graphic because selecting it opens the resource to which it points. Instead, right-click the hyperlink, choose the shortcut menu's Hyperlink command, and then choose the submenu's Remove Hyperlink command.

CHAPTER 3

Word Basics

Using **Microsoft Word 2000**, you can create **documents** that you intend to print and distribute. You can create **web pages.** You can create **e-mail** messages, fax cover sheets, and calendars—in short, you can create just about any kind of document you can think of, from legal pleadings to a newsletter. Some publishers use Word as a desktop publishing **program**, creating and formatting entire books and magazines that they send directly to a commercial printer.

Regardless of the type of document you need to produce, the basics are the same, and in this chapter we'll look at all of them:

- Creating a Word document
- Working with different **views**
- Adding text and pictures
- Formatting a document
- Editing in Word

Creating a Word Document

You create a document in the **document window**, which is contained within Word's **program window**. The Word document window is similar in some respects to other Microsoft Office document windows, but it includes some special features, as shown in Figure 3-1.

We've already looked at the features of the document window that are common to all Office programs, so this chapter describes only the View buttons and the Browse buttons. You can display a Word document in four views, which are explained in the later section "Working with Different Views." This section introduces the Browse buttons.

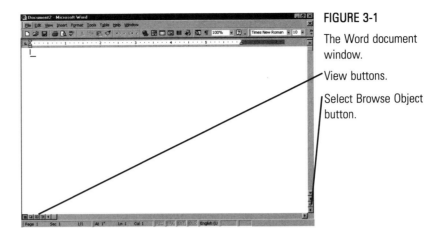

FIGURE 3-1

The Word document window.

View buttons.

Select Browse Object button.

Clicking the Previous Page button displays the previous page of a document, and clicking the Next Page button displays the next page of a document. Clicking the Select Browse Object button, however, opens the **menu** shown in Figure 3-2.

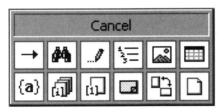

FIGURE 3-2

The Browse menu.

In Word, an **object** is any one of the following: a field, an endnote, a footnote, a comment, a section, a page, an edit, a heading, a graphic, or a **table.** To browse by object simply means selecting a type of object and then moving through a document from one of these objects to the next. After you select an object, simply click the Previous button or the Next button to go to the next object. (After you select an object, the Previous Page or Next Page buttons change to specify the object, for example, Previous Table, Next Comment.) When you browse by any object other than page, the Previous and Next buttons turn blue to remind you that another object is active. Browsing objects can be quite handy when you're working with long documents.

Notes *Don't worry if you aren't familiar with some of these object types. This chapter and the next include explanations.*

Starting from Scratch

To create a simple document, such as a letter to a friend or a short memo, just open Word and start typing. Text automatically wraps to the next line when you reach the right margin. To start a new paragraph, press the Enter key. To correct a typing error, press the Backspace or Delete key, or click the Undo toolbar button.

You'll also find it helpful to know about and use the keys described in Table 3-1. These special keys are called navigation keys, and you use them to move around a document quickly.

Press	To Go To
Home	The beginning of the current line.
End	The end of the current line.
Ctrl+Home	The beginning of the document.
Ctrl+End	The end of the document.
Page Up	The previous screen.
Page Down	The next screen.
Ctrl+Page Up	The top of the screen.
Ctrl+Page Down	The bottom of the screen.
Alt+Left Arrow	One word to the left.
Alt+Right Arrow	One word to the right.

TABLE 3-1: The navigation keys.

 In a key sequence such as Ctrl+Home, hold down the first key and press the second key.

This is all you really need to know to create a simple document from scratch in Word. As you create and work with long documents and documents for special purposes, you'll want to take advantage of a couple of indispensable Word features: **styles** and **document templates.** The later section, "Working with Styles," talks about styles, but first let's look at Word's templates.

Using a Template

A document template is a collection of formatting options (and sometimes content) that is available when you create a new document. When you open Word and just start typing, you are using the Normal template. This template comes with Word, and you use it automatically if you haven't selected one of the many other templates that also come with Word.

The Normal template includes only a few simple formats: the **font** style and size of regular text, and three levels of headings. To see these, click the Style drop-down list on the **Personal toolbar.** Your list should look like the one in Figure 3-3.

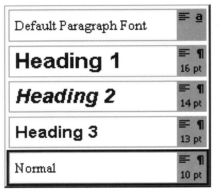

FIGURE 3-3

The styles available in the Normal template.

When you create a new document, however, you can choose from among many other templates. Choose the File menu's New command to display the New **dialog box**, as shown in Figure 3-4, and survey your choices.

FIGURE 3-4

The New dialog box.

The tabs in the New dialog box indicate the categories of templates you can choose from. Take a minute to click through the tabs to get an idea of what's available. You'll notice that in addition to templates, you can choose a **wizard**, which walks you through the steps to customize a preformatted document. Figure 3-5 shows the first step in the Fax Wizard, which walks you through the process of creating a cover sheet and then faxing a document.

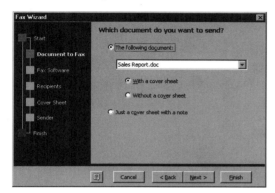

FIGURE 3-5

You can also open the Fax Wizard by choosing the File menu's Send To command and the submenu's Fax Recipient command.

A template is preformatted and often includes placeholders where you can insert your text. It also contains instructions for using the template. When you select a template, the Preview box displays a miniature of it. Figure 3-6 shows the Brochure template, chosen from the Publications tab. It opens in Print Layout view (which the next section covers).

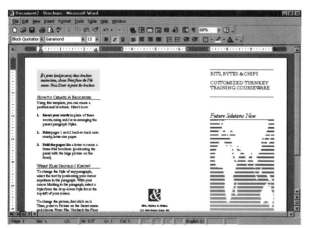

FIGURE 3-6

The Brochure template has a three-column layout, which you then print and fold in thirds.

To use a template, simply replace the placeholder text and pictures with those of your own. If you have a document format that you often use, you can save it as a template. To do this, follow these steps:

1 Choose the File menu's Save As command to display the Save As dialog box.

2 Select **Document Template** (*.dot) from the Save As Type drop-down list box.

3 Select the Templates **folder,** and enter a name for the template.

4 Click Save.

Working with Different Views

In Word, you can display a document in six views:

- Normal
- Web Layout
- Print Layout
- Outline
- Print Preview
- Full Screen

Figures 3-7 through 3-10 show the same document in four of the views. The easiest way to display one of these views is to click a View button in the lower left of the screen, as shown in Figure 3-1. Rest the mouse pointer over a button to display its name in a ScreenTip.

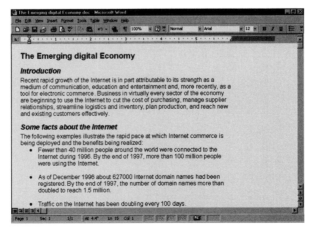

FIGURE 3-7

Normal view.

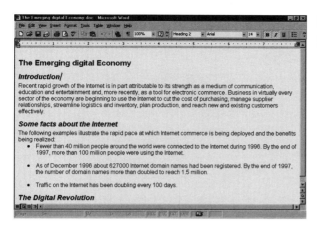

FIGURE 3-8

Web Layout view.

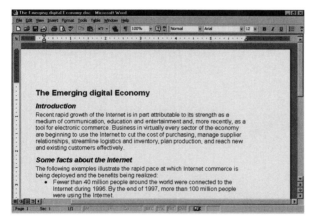

FIGURE 3-9

Print Layout view.

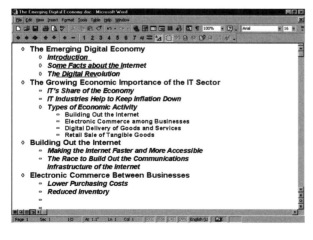

FIGURE 3-10

Outline view.

Each view is best suited for a specific display and for a particular kind of work:

- Normal: Use this view for entering, editing, and formatting text. Headers, footers, graphics, and columns are not visible in Normal view.

- Web Layout: This view displays your document as it will appear in a **web browser.** There are no page breaks, and text and tables wrap to fit in the window.

- Print Layout: This view displays the document exactly as it will appear when printed. (In previous versions of Word, this view was called Page Layout.)

- Outline: You can use this view when initially structuring a document or to see and rearrange headings and sections of a document while you are working on it. (It's a good practice to create an outline before composing a document of any length.)

Notes *Chapter 4 describes the details of working in Outline view.*

- Print Preview: Use this view to display the document as a full page or as multiple full pages. For more information about Print Preview, see Chapter 2.

- Full Screen: Use this view if you want to display only the document itself, not the **toolbars, ruler,** title bar, and so on. To display a document in Full Screen view, choose the View menu's Full Screen command. To return to the view that was displayed before you chose Full Screen, press the Esc key.

Adding Text and Pictures

In the first section of this chapter, we looked at how to create some simple documents by entering text or replacing placeholder text with your own text. But your documents can contain more than text, and you can use some special features of Word to enter certain kinds of text.

Typing Text

Chapter 2 mentions **Click-and-Type,** a feature that's new in Word 2000. The advantage of Click-and-Type is that you can enter text (or a picture, for that matter) anywhere on the page, not just at the **insertion point.** To use Click-and-Type, display your document in Print Layout or Web Layout view, and then simply **double-click** anywhere on the page.

For example, if you want to center a title for your document on a title page, double-click in the center of the page and start typing. Experiment with Click-and-Type to see the possibilities, and notice the special insertion point that Word uses.

 To see how much text you've typed in a document, choose the Tools menu's Word Count command. Word displays the Word Count dialog box, which lists the number of pages, words, characters, paragraphs, and lines in the document.

If you often insert the same content in many of your documents, you'll want to take advantage of Word's **AutoText** feature. For example, if you have boilerplate copyright information that you add to all your documents, you can create an AutoText entry for it. Then, rather than typing it every time or even **copying** it from another document, you can simply type its short name, and Word automatically enters the text.

 You can also store graphics as AutoText entries. You might want to do this if you always insert your company logo in your documents.

To create an AutoText entry, follow these steps:

1 Select the text or graphic for which you want to create an AutoText entry.

2 Choose the Insert menu's AutoText command, and then choose the submenu's New command to display the Create AutoText dialog box, as shown in Figure 3-11.

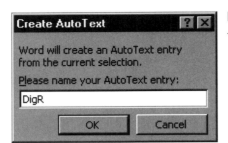

FIGURE 3-11

Type a name for your AutoText entry.

3 Enter a name for your AutoText entry, and click OK.

To insert your AutoText entry, type its name and press the F3 key.

Word comes with a number of AutoText entries that you can use. To see the list, choose the Insert menu's AutoText command. Click a category to select from a list of entries for that category.

You can also choose the Insert menu's AutoText command and choose AutoText to display the AutoCorrect dialog box. Click the AutoText tab. You can use this tab to insert an AutoText entry and to delete an entry; click Show Toolbar to display the AutoText toolbar. If you are creating a number of entries, you might find it more convenient to display and use the toolbar.

Inserting Symbols

Many symbols that you might use often in Word are not on the standard keyboard—a registered mark (®), the copyright symbol (©), a division sign (÷), and so on. You can enter a few of these using **AutoCorrect**, as described in Chapter 2. The Symbol dialog box, however, provides a rich array of characters that you can easily insert in your documents.

To insert a symbol in Word, follow these steps:

1 Place the insertion point in your document where you want to insert the symbol.

2 Choose the Insert menu's Symbol command to display the Symbol dialog box, as shown in Figure 3-12.

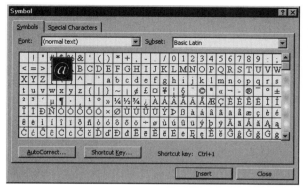

FIGURE 3-12

The Symbol dialog box with the @ sign selected.

3 By default, the Symbols tab is selected and the Normal Text font is selected in the Font drop-down list. To insert a symbol, simply double-click it, and then click Close.

To get a sense of the huge variety of symbols at your disposal, select various fonts from the Font drop-down list box and notice how the display of symbols changes. In addition, you can select a font and then select from the Subset drop-down list box to display even more symbols. If a symbol has an associated shortcut key, Word displays its shortcut key in the lower right corner. If a symbol does not have a shortcut key and you want to assign one, click Shortcut Key to display the Customize Keyboard dialog box, as shown in Figure 3-13. Press a shortcut key combination, such as Ctrl+1, and click Assign. If the key combination is already chosen, Word displays that information below the Press New Shortcut Key box.

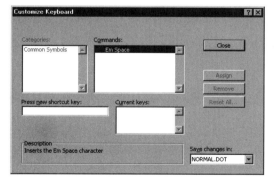

FIGURE 3-13

Press a new shortcut key to assign it to a symbol.

You can insert some symbols using the Special Characters tab, as shown in Figure 3-14. Simply double-click a symbol name to insert it, and then click Close.

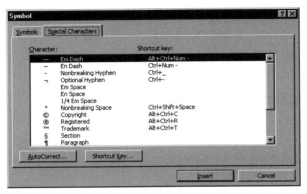

FIGURE 3-14

Drag the scrollbar to see the entire list of special characters and their assigned shortcut keys.

Inserting Pictures

You can often significantly enhance a Word document with visual images. If you have a collection of your own digital art, you can insert one of those **files.** To do so, follow these steps:

1 Click to place the insertion point in the document where you want the picture.

2 Choose the Insert menu's Picture command, and choose the submenu's From File command to display the Insert Picture dialog box.

3 Select a folder and a file, and click Insert.

You can also select an image from the Clip Art Gallery. To do so, follow these steps:

1 Click to place the insertion point in the document where you want the picture.

2 Choose the Insert menu's Picture command, and then choose the submenu's Clip Art command to display the Insert ClipArt dialog box, as shown in Figure 3-15.

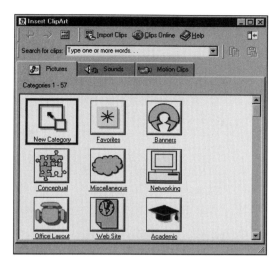

FIGURE 3-15

Use this dialog box to select a picture, sound, or motion clip.

3 Click the Pictures tab.

4 Click a category icon, browse to select a picture, and then click it to open a pop-up shortcut menu.

5 Click Insert Clip to insert the picture in your document.

When you select a picture in your document, Word adds the Picture toolbar to the program window. You can use the Picture toolbar's buttons to edit the image. To display the Picture toolbar, right-click the picture and choose the shortcut menu's Show Picture Toolbar command.

Copying Text from Other Documents

You can copy text from another Word document into the current document, or you can copy text from any other Office program into a Word document. To do so, follow these steps:

1 Select the text you want to copy, and choose the Edit menu's Copy command or press Ctrl+C.

2 Place the insertion point in the document where you want to insert the text, and then choose the Edit menu's Paste command or press Ctrl+V.

Formatting a Document

Formatting a document means specifying how it looks. You can format a document on three levels: character, paragraph, and page. When you format characters, you determine the font in which they are displayed, the font's style and size, its color, and any special effect, such as superscript or small caps. When you format a paragraph, you specify the line spacing, first line indentation, alignment, and the spacing before and after the paragraph. When you format a page, you specify its top, bottom, left, and right margins and such things as where the pages break.

The formatting tool you use depends on what you are formatting.

Using the Formatting Toolbar

As mentioned in earlier chapters of this book, the Standard and Formatting toolbars are combined into the Personal toolbar in Office 2000, and the Personal toolbar is displayed on one row. When you're working in Word, you might want to display the Formatting toolbar on a separate row. For instructions on how to do this, see "Using the Personal Toolbar" in Chapter 2.

When you display the Formatting toolbar on a separate row, it contains the buttons shown in Figure 3-16. Point to a button to display its name and shortcut keys in a ScreenTip.

FIGURE 3-16

The Formatting toolbar.

Table 3-2 lists and describes the buttons on the Formatting toolbar.

Button	What It Does
Style	Applies a style to selected text.
Font	Applies a font to selected text.
Font Size	Applies a font size to selected text.
Bold	Formats selected text in boldface type.
Italic	Formats selected text in italics.
Underline	Underlines selected text.
Align Left	Aligns selected text with the left margin.
Center	Centers selected text horizontally between the left and right margins.
Align Right	Aligns selected text with the right margin.
Justify	Aligns selected text with both the left and right margins.
Numbering	Applies a numbered list style to selected text.
Bullets	Applies a bulleted list style to selected text.
Decrease Indent	Decreases the paragraph indentation by 0.5 inch.
Increase Indent	Increases the paragraph indentation by 0.5 inch.
Outside Border	Opens a drop-down list from which you can choose a border for selected text.
Highlight	Lets you select a highlight color to apply to selected text.
Font Color	Lets you select a color to apply to selected text.

TABLE 3-2: The Formatting toolbar buttons (from left to right).

You can apply formatting as you type, or you can compose your document and then format. When you click a Formatting toolbar button and then type, Word applies the button's style to everything you type until you click the button again.

 You can also apply character formatting using the Font dialog box. Just select the text you want to format, choose the Format menu's Font command, make your choices, and click OK.

Using the Ruler

Although you can get by in Word without using the ruler (there are other ways to take care of the same tasks), it is often the most straightforward way to set margins, indentations, and tabs. And, of course, many people prefer a visual tool such as the ruler. The horizontal ruler is displayed in Normal and Web Layout views. Both the horizontal and vertical rulers are displayed in Print Layout view.

As Figure 3-17 shows, the ruler contains four indent markers. To change any of them, simply **drag** the marker.

Tab Selection button   Left Indent Hanging Indent   First Line Indent Right Indent

FIGURE 3-17

Set indentations using the ruler.

- The First Line Indent marker indicates where the first line of paragraphs will start.
- The Hanging Indent marker indicates if, and where, successive lines in a paragraph will indent to the right of the first line indent.
- The Left Indent marker indicates the left margin.
- The Right Indent marker indicates the right margin.

In almost every case, there is a better way to do something in Word besides using tabs. (Usually, you can use tables, which are described in the next chapter.) You can, however, set tabs with the ruler. At the far left edge of the ruler is a Tab Selection button. You have four tab choices: Left, Center, Decimal, and Bar. Simply click the Tab Selection button to toggle through these choices. To set tabs using the ruler, follow these steps:

1 Select a tab type.

2 Click on the ruler to set the tab stop. All default stops to the left of the new tab are deleted.

3 Drag the tab marker to change the tab position.

To remove a tab stop, drag it off the ruler.

Creating Page Breaks

Word automatically creates page breaks as you compose a document. In Normal view, Word indicates a page break by a horizontal line. In Print Layout view, Word indicates a page break by a solid dark gray shadow that appears between pages. Word estimates where to break pages according to the rules established in the Paragraph dialog box, as shown in Figure 3-18. To display this dialog box, choose the Format menu's Paragraph command. Click the Line And Page Breaks tab.

FIGURE 3-18

Some of the settings in the Line And Page Breaks tab determine where pages break.

If the Widow/Orphan Control check box is selected, Word does not allow the first line of a paragraph to end a page (an orphan), nor does it allow the last line of a paragraph to appear as the first line on a page (a widow). To keep specific lines of text or paragraphs together rather than being broken across two pages, select them and select the Keep Lines Together check box. If you don't want Word to break pages between a heading and its text, select the heading and select the Keep With Next check box.

You can override Word's pagination by inserting manual page breaks. One way to do this is to position the insertion point in your document, open the Paragraph dialog box at the Line And Page Breaks tab, and select the Page Break Before check box. It's much easier, however, to position the insertion point and press Ctrl+Enter.

A quick way to check page breaks in a document is to look at the pages in Print Preview.

Adding Page Numbers

You can add page numbers in a Word document in two ways: by using the Page Numbers dialog box and by formatting headers and footers. If you want to add only page numbers and not any additional information such as the date or document title, use the Page Numbers dialog box. To do so, follow these steps:

1 With the document open, choose the Insert menu's Page Numbers command to display the Page Numbers dialog box, as shown in Figure 3-19.

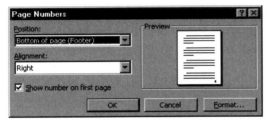

FIGURE 3-19

Format page numbers using the Page Numbers dialog box.

2 Select the page number position from the Position drop-down list box.

3 Select the page number alignment from the Alignment drop-down list box.

4 If you don't want a number on the first page (and you probably don't), clear the Show Number On First Page check box.

5 To specify a numbering style or to indicate that you want to include a chapter number with the page number, click Format to display the Page Number Format dialog box, as shown in Figure 3-20.

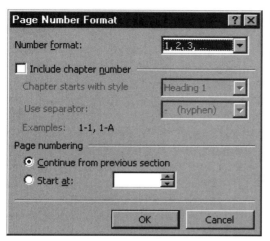

FIGURE 3-20

The Page Number Format dialog box.

6 To use a number format other than standard arabic, select an entry from the Number Format drop-down list box.

7 To include a chapter number, select the Include Chapter Number check box, and indicate the style that is attached to the chapter number and specify a separator to be used between the chapter and page number.

8 Click an option button to indicate whether you want to continue the numbering from the previous section or to start numbering over at a certain number.

9 Click OK, and then click OK again in the Page Numbers dialog box.

Using headers and footers to insert page numbers is a bit more involved, but it's certainly something you'll want to know about sooner or later. For all the details, open Help and search on Header.

Working with Styles

Styles are one of the biggest time-savers for people who create or work with lots of documents. In addition, by using styles, you can create a consistent look to all your documents or to all the documents produced by your organization or company. A style is simply a collection of formats that you can apply with a couple of mouse clicks and can include fonts, sizes, font attributes, alignment, character spacing, paragraph spacing, bullets and numbering, borders, indentation, and just about any other formatting you can think of.

Earlier in this chapter, in the discussion about templates, we took a quick look at the styles in the Normal template. To look at this from yet another perspective, open a document that you've created using styles (perhaps those in the Normal template), choose the Help menu's What's This? command, and click a paragraph or a heading. You'll see a listing of all the pertinent formatting contained in the applied style in a comment balloon, as shown in Figure 3-21. You can easily see that applying a style is much more efficient than selecting and applying each of those formats to every paragraph you create.

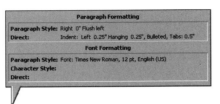

FIGURE 3-21

These are all the styles applied in this paragraph.

Entire books have been devoted to Word styles, so this little one obviously can't go into everything you'll ever need to know about styles. However, let's briefly discuss one way that you can quickly and easily create a style of your own, and then modify the style.

To create a style, follow these steps:

1 Create a paragraph or a heading that contains all the formatting you want to apply, including font, font size, alignment, any enhancements, and so on.

2 Be sure the insertion point is within the paragraph or heading, and click the Style toolbar box to select it.

3 Type a name for your style, and press the Enter key.

That's all there is to it. Click the Style box's drop-down arrow to see your style displayed in the list. You can now use it just as you use any of the other styles in the list.

To modify a style you've created, follow these steps:

1   Choose the Format menu's Style command to display the Style dialog box, as shown in Figure 3-22.

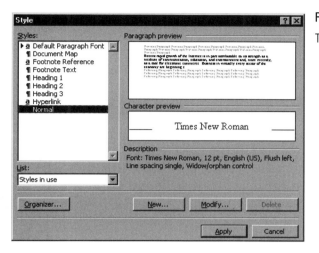

FIGURE 3-22

The Style dialog box.

2   Select the style you want to modify from the Styles list, and click Modify to display the Modify Style dialog box, as shown in Figure 3-23.

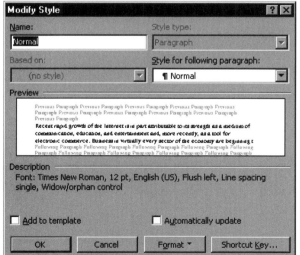

FIGURE 3-23

The Modify Style dialog box.

3 Use the options in the Modify Style dialog box to adjust your style. If you want to change the formatting, click Format, select the attribute you want to change, and make the change in the dialog box that is displayed. When you're finished, click OK.

4 In the Modify Style dialog box, click OK.

5 Back in the Style dialog box, click Apply. Now Word reformats all text formatted with that style to conform to the modified style.

Working with Themes

If you use Word to create web pages, you'll probably want to take advantage of the more than 30 design **themes** that are new to Office 2000. You can apply a theme after you create a document, or you can open a new document, select a theme, and then work in it as you create the document. In either case, to use a theme, follow these steps:

1 Open a new document or an existing one.

2 Choose the Format menu's Theme command to display the Theme dialog box, as shown in Figure 3-24.

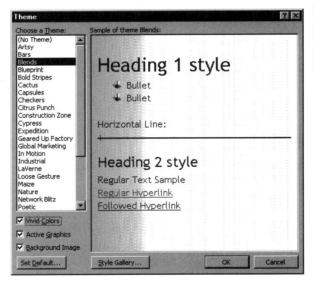

FIGURE 3-24

Select a theme from the list on the left to see a preview in the pane on the right.

3 Select the Vivid Colors check box to display the theme in more brilliant colors.

4 To turn off Active Graphics, clear the Active Graphics check box.

5 To eliminate a background image, clear the Background Image check box.

6 If you also want to select a template, click Style Gallery to display the Style Gallery dialog box. Select a template, and click OK.

7 If you don't want to select a template, simply click OK to apply the theme to your document.

Notes *Not all themes are installed when you install Word. If you select a theme that is not installed, you might see the message "To install the selected theme and see its preview, click Install." You'll need to insert the installation CD-ROM in the CD-ROM drive to install the theme.*

Editing in Word

If you are creating a document for anything other than a personal journal, you want it to appear as polished and professional as it possibly can. Fortunately, Word includes several tools that you can use to review and polish your documents, including a highlighter, a Find and Replace tool, a spelling and grammar checker, and also a revision marker.

Highlighting Text

If you're in the habit of using a colored highlighter pen as you review printed reports or study manuals or other books, you'll probably want to use Word's highlighter. To use Word's highlighter, click the down arrow beside the Highlight toolbar button (see Figure 3-25), select a color, and then drag over text in your document to highlight it. To turn off highlighting, simply click the Highlight button again. The next time you want to highlight, simply click the Highlight button if you want to use the same color again. If you have a color printer, the text is also highlighted when printed.

FIGURE 3-25
The Highlight toolbar button.

Using Find and Replace

The Find feature locates text, and the Replace feature substitutes new text for the existing text. To use Find and Replace, follow these steps:

1 Click the Select Browse Object button, and click the Find button to display the Find And Replace dialog box.

2 Click More to display all the search options, and then click the Replace tab, as shown in Figure 3-26.

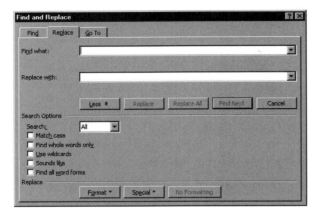

FIGURE 3-26

The Replace tab of the Find And Replace dialog box.

3 In the Find What text box, enter the text you want to locate.

4 In the Replace With text box, enter the substitution text.

5 In the Search Options section, specify additional criteria for the text you want to locate.

6 In the Replace section, click Format if the text you want to replace is in a certain font, style, language, and so on.

7 If you want to find a special character, such as a paragraph mark, a page break, or a tab, click Special and select from the list.

8 After you specify your options, click Replace, Replace All, or Find Next.

Wildcards *are characters that stand for any character. A question mark stands for any single character and an asterisk for any string of characters. For example, if you enter* s*, *you'll locate all words that start with* s. *If you enter* *ed, *you'll find all words that end with* ed.

A Reminder About the Spell Checker

By default, Word checks spelling as you type, placing a red wavy line beneath any misspelled words. If you prefer to check spelling all at once, you can turn off this feature. Choose the Tools menu's Options command, and click the Spelling & Grammar tab. Clear the Check Spelling As You Type check box, and click OK.

Now to check the spelling in your document, choose the Tools menu's Spelling And Grammar command (or click the Spelling And Grammar button on the Personal toolbar). When Word finds a misspelled word, it displays a dialog box similar to that in Figure 3-27. If you want to accept word's suggestion for a correction, click Change.

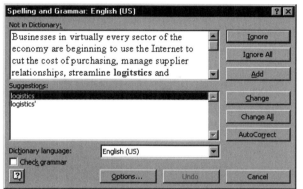

FIGURE 3-27

The Spelling And Grammar dialog box.

Here's how the other buttons in this dialog box work:

- Clicking Ignore ignores the current spelling and finds the next misspelled word.
- Clicking Ignore All ignores any other words that are spelled in exactly the same way. (You often click Ignore All to tell Word to ignore proper names in the spelling check.)
- Clicking Add adds the word to the current dictionary.
- Clicking Change All changes all spellings of the current word to the suggested correction or the correction you specify.
- Clicking AutoCorrect adds the word to the list of words that Word automatically corrects as you type.

By default, Word automatically detects the language in which you're writing and uses this language to spell-check your text. To set the language of selected text manually, choose the Tools menu's Language command and then choose the submenu's Set Language command.

Using the Grammar Checker

If you want to check grammar as well as spelling in a document, select
the Check Grammar As You Type check box in the Spelling & Grammar
tab. To display this tab, click Options in the Spelling And Grammar
dialog box, or choose the Tools menu's Options command, and then
click the Spelling & Grammar tab.

 *To replace a word with one of Word's synonyms, right-click the word
and choose the shortcut menu's Synonyms command. Then select a
synonym from the list.*

Using Revision Marks

If more than one person works on a document, you'll probably want to
track all the changes. Each person's changes will appear in a different
color, and you can use formatting to tell what has been added, what has
been deleted, and even what has been reformatted. To track changes,
choose the Tools menu's Track Changes command and choose the
submenu's Highlight Changes command to display the Highlight
Changes dialog box, as shown in Figure 3-28. Select the Track Changes
While Editing check box.

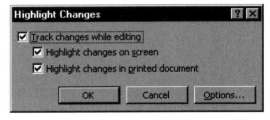

FIGURE 3-28

The Highlight Changes dialog box.

By default, Word cycles through 15 colors to identify changes. In other
words, as many as 15 people can edit the document before Word starts
reusing a color. If you want to specify other color arrangements or if you
want to change the way Word formats changes (by default, added text is
underlined and deleted text is struck through), click Options in the
Highlight Changes dialog box to display the Track Changes dialog box,
as shown in Figure 3-29. Select entries from the drop-down list boxes to
specify different color arrangements or alter the formatting of changes.

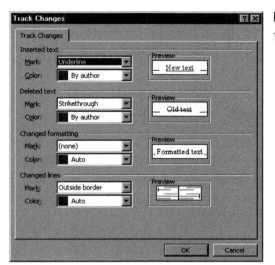

FIGURE 3-29

The Track Changes dialog box.

To review changes and accept or reject them, choose the Tools menu's Track Changes command and then choose the submenu's Accept Or Reject Changes command to display the Accept Or Reject Changes dialog box. To go through the changes, click one of the Find buttons. When Word finds a change, it highlights the change in the document and displays a note in the Accept Or Reject Changes dialog box about who made the change, the type of change, and the date and time it was made.

Adding Comments

To annotate a Word document with comments, you can use Word's Comment feature. To insert a comment, follow these steps:

1 Select the text on which you want to comment.

2 Choose the Insert menu's Comment command. Word highlights your selection in yellow, adds your initials to the highlighted text, and displays the Comments pane at the bottom of the window, as shown in Figure 3-30.

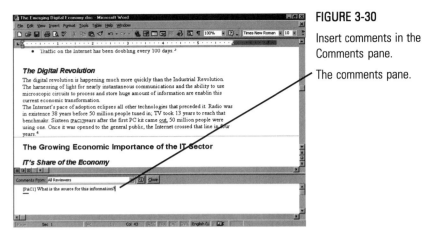

FIGURE 3-30

Insert comments in the Comments pane.

The comments pane.

3 Enter your comment in the Comments pane, and click Close to close the pane.

To view the comment associated with a text selection, rest the mouse over the highlighted and initialed text. Word displays a ScreenTip that names the person who added the comment and lists the text of the comment. You can also view all of a document's comments in the Comments pane by choosing the View menu's Comments command. To edit a comment, right-click the highlighted text and choose the shortcut menu's Edit Comment command. To delete a comment, right-click the highlighted text and choose the shortcut menu's Delete Comment command.

CHAPTER 4

Beyond Word Basics

Now that we've looked at what you need to know to do basic work in **Microsoft Word 2000,** we can look at some more advanced features. I call these features "more advanced," not because they are more difficult, but because they are not features that you necessarily use every day. For example, not every **document** you create can benefit from a **table,** but you definitely want to know how and when to create a table. The same goes for columns, **text boxes,** and **mail merge.** This chapter steps you through the following:

- Working with tables
- Outlining with Word
- Advanced layout options
- Using mail merge
- Working with special document elements

Working with Tables

A table is simply a format for presenting information in rows and columns. A table is the best way to present information such as a contact list for people in your organization (names, addresses, phone numbers, and **e-mail** addresses); a list that contains data you might want to calculate (sales territories, quarterly goals for each territory, and the total estimated revenue); or even a glossary. You can insert pictures or graphics in a table, and you can format a table with shading, colors, borders, and so on. Figure 4-1 shows a simple table created to keep track of the people in an organization. Periodically, it is updated and sent to people in the group as an e-mail **attachment.** (Chapter 6 describes how to send an e-mail attachment.)

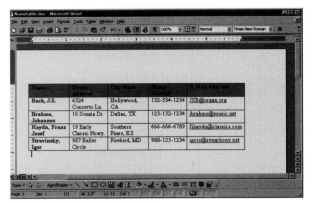

FIGURE 4-1

Use a table when you want to display information that is similar to this.

 You can also place information in tables and then get rid of the gridlines so that your table appears as parallel columns. (Faint vertical gridlines are still displayed onscreen, but not on printouts.) In this book, tables have only horizontal gridlines, and you can use Word to format tables in that way also.

Creating Tables

The simplest way to create a table is to **click** the Insert Table button on the **Personal toolbar,** move the pointer over the grid (shown in Figure 4-2), and click to indicate the number of rows and columns you want. Word displays the table in your document. Don't worry if you change your mind and want more or fewer rows and columns; you can easily add and delete them at any time.

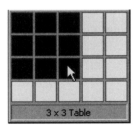

FIGURE 4-2

Use this grid to create a table.

A **cell** is the place in a table where a row and column intersect, and you enter data in cells. To do so, simply click in a cell and start typing. To move to the next cell, press the Tab key. Table 4-1 lists the other navigation keys for tables.

Press	To Go To
Shift+Tab	The previous cell.
Alt+End	The last cell in a row.
Alt+Home	The first cell in a row.
Alt+Page Down	The last cell in a column.
Alt+Page Up	The first cell in a column.

TABLE **4-1**: Navigation keys for use with tables.

To add a row or column, place the **insertion point** in a cell and choose the Table **menu's** Insert command. Then choose the appropriate command from the submenu. To delete a row or column, place the insertion point in a cell and choose the Table menu's Delete command. Then choose the appropriate command from the submenu.

Formatting a Table

You can format a table in myriad ways using the Tables And Borders **toolbar,** as shown in Figure 4-3. To display this toolbar, right-click any toolbar and choose the shortcut menu's Tables And Borders command. However, here I'm going to show you the quick and easy way: letting Word do the formatting.

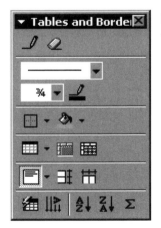

FIGURE **4-3**

The Tables And Borders toolbar.

When you "let Word do the formatting," you use the AutoFormat command. To use AutoFormat, follow these steps:

1 Click in your table.

2 Choose the Table menu's Table AutoFormat command to display the Table AutoFormat **dialog box**, as shown in Figure 4-4.

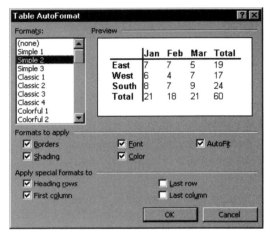

FIGURE 4-4

Click a format to see what it looks like in the Preview box.

3 Select a format and experiment with the options in the Formats To Apply section and the Apply Special Formats To section until you see the look you want in the Preview box.

4 Click OK when you're satisfied with the look of your table.

You can use all the buttons on the Formatting toolbar to format the cells in a table. You can also use buttons on the Tables And Borders toolbar to format the cells in a table. For example, you can rotate the text in a cell by selecting the text and clicking the Change Text Direction button. You can remove the gridlines from a table by selecting the table, clicking the Outside Border button, and selecting the option that has no gridlines.

Outlining with Word

Chapter 3 mentions that Outline **view** is one of the ways to display your work in Word. This chapter demonstrates how you use the Outlining toolbar and introduces you to some features that come in handy when you work with long documents that have multiple headings.

You are probably aware that any time you create a long document you really should construct an outline first. Most of us like to skip this step in the writing process, but that's usually a mistake. Preparing an outline is the best way to organize your thoughts, and by using Word's Outlining feature, you can go a step farther and easily reorganize your thoughts to your heart's content.

Creating a Document in Outline View

To create a document in Outline view, choose the View menu's Outline command. This displays the Outlining toolbar, as shown in Figure 4-5. If you're using the Personal toolbar, the Outlining toolbar appears directly beneath it. Point to a button to display its name.

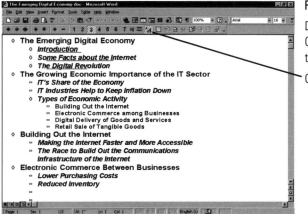

FIGURE 4-5

Displaying a document in Outline view also displays the Outlining toolbar.

Outlining toolbar.

Use the buttons on the left side of the toolbar to promote and demote outline levels, to move text up or down, and to expand or collapse headings. Use the numbered buttons and the All button to specify the number of levels you want to display.

You'll no doubt start creating your outline using a Level 1 heading. After you enter the text for that heading, you can press the Enter key to enter another Level 1 heading, or you can press the Enter key and then press the Tab key or click the Demote toolbar button to enter a Level 2 heading.

You may remember from student days that a good outline doesn't necessarily need several heading levels; it might have only Level 1s and Level 2s. However, regardless of the number of levels, you always need at least two of each level you use. For example, you don't want a Level 1 heading, a Level 2 heading, and then another Level 1 heading. You need at least two Level 2 headings between the Level 1 headings.

Reorganizing an Outline

To move text in an outline, use the Move Up and Move Down toolbar buttons. When you move a heading, the accompanying text moves with it. To reorganize an outline, follow these steps:

1 Click the heading you want to move.

2 To also move any subheadings under the heading, click the Collapse toolbar button.

3 To move only the heading and its accompanying text, click the Expand toolbar button.

4 Click the Move Up or Move Down toolbar button until the heading appears where you want it.

 To print an outline, display what you want to print on the screen and click the Print toolbar button.

Advanced Layout Options

If you do any sort of desktop publishing, you'll want to know about and use columns, text boxes, and captions. If you're following this chapter along at your computer, be sure that you're now in Print Layout view or Web Layout view. You can't see the effects of these layout options in Normal view.

Using Columns

Newspapers, magazines, and often reference books such as encyclopedias and dictionaries print text in columns. One reason they do so is that you can get more text on a page using columns.

 Don't use columns if text in one column refers to text in the other, for example, as a schedule might. For that, use a table and then remove the gridlines.

You can enter text and then format it in columns, or you can set up your column layout and then enter text. In either case, to format columns, follow these steps:

1 Place the insertion point where you want the first column to begin.

2 Choose the Format menu's Columns command to display the Columns dialog box, as shown in Figure 4-6.

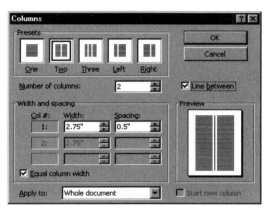

FIGURE 4-6

In the Columns dialog box, specify the number of columns, the width, the spacing, and whether you want a line between columns.

3 Select one of the preset column layouts, or select a number in the Number Of Columns box.

4 In the Width And Spacing section, specify the width of each column and the spacing between columns, or simply select the Equal Column Width check box if you want all the columns the same width across the page.

5 If you want lines to separate columns, select the Line Between check box.

6 In the Apply To drop-down list box, specify what part of the document you want to format in columns.

7 Click OK.

If you aren't happy with the way Word breaks the columns, you can insert your own breaks. Place the insertion point where you want a column to break, choose the Insert menu's Break command, and in the Break dialog box, click the Column Break option button. If you change your mind and decide that you don't want columns after all, choose the Format menu's Columns command, and in the Columns dialog box, select the One preset option, and click OK.

Sometimes a neat way to enhance the layout of columns is to create a headline that spans two or more columns. You do this using a text box, which leads us to the topic of the next section.

Using Text Boxes

You can use a text box to create a headline, an announcement that you want to place in the middle of a page, or anything else that you want to stand out from the rest of the text. A big advantage to using text boxes is that you can place them where you want them and anchor them to that spot if you don't want them to flow with the text. You can also create special effects for the text in a text box, using, for example, **WordArt** (as described in Chapter 2 in the section "Using the Office Drawing Tools") or the Change Text Direction button on the Tables And Borders toolbar.

To create a text box, follow these steps:

1   Place the insertion point where you want to insert the text box.

 *You can use **Click-and-Type** to insert a text box, as long as you don't have more than one column. Simply **double-click** anywhere on the screen where you want the text box.*

2   Choose the Insert menu's Text Box command.

3   The pointer changes to a cross. Now click in what will become the upper left corner of the text box, and **drag** to the opposite corner. Lines appear as you drag.

4   Release the mouse button, and your text box appears outlined by hash marks and with sizing handles, as shown in Figure 4-7.

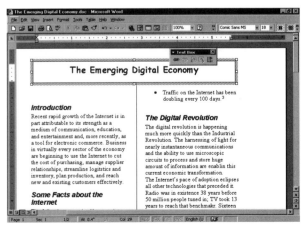

FIGURE 4-7

Enter your text in the text box.

5 Enter your text in the text box. Click outside the text box to remove the sizing handles and display the text and the borders of your text box.

To format your text box, select it and double-click a border to display the Format Text Box dialog box. Use the Colors And Lines tab to specify a fill color and a color and style for the border lines. Use the Layout tab, as shown in Figure 4-8, to specify how text will wrap around your text box.

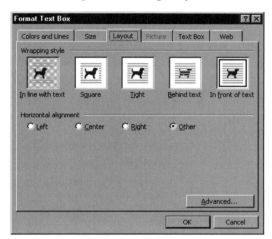

FIGURE 4-8

The Layout tab of the Format Text Box dialog box.

If you want your text box to stay exactly where you inserted it instead of moving with text, in the Layout tab click Advanced to display the Advanced Layout dialog box. Click the Picture Position tab, and select the Lock Anchor check box.

To change the dimensions of a text box, follow these steps:

1 Click in the text box to select it.

2 Move the pointer over a handle.

3 To change the size and proportions, drag a sizing handle on the side of the text box.

4 To change the size but not the proportions, drag a sizing handle in the corner of the text box.

To move a text box, place the pointer over the perimeter of the text box but not over a sizing handle, and drag the text box to a new location.

 To delete a text box, click on the perimeter of the text box and press the Delete key or choose the Edit menu's Clear command.

Before I leave this section, I want to describe how to insert a headline over columns. To do this, follow these steps:

1 Place the insertion point at the top of the first column where you want to insert the heading.

2 Choose the Insert menu's Text Box command, and draw the text box so it extends over two or more column widths.

3 Enter the headline text.

4 With the text box still selected, double-click the perimeter to display the Format Text Box dialog box, and click the Layout tab.

5 Select the Square wrapping style, and click OK. Your headline now appears above the columns.

Adding Captions

In Word, you can add a caption, like the one shown in Figure 4-9, to equations, figures, tables, graphics, pictures, special text such as program lines, and so on. Word even numbers captions automatically.

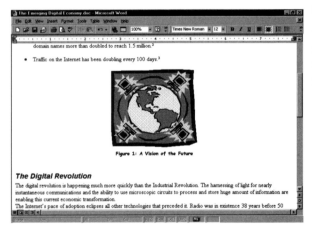

FIGURE 4-9

Use Word's Caption command to insert captions in your documents.

To insert a caption, follow these steps:

1 Select what you want to caption—a graphic, a picture, a table, and so on.

2 Choose the Insert menu's Caption command to display the Caption dialog box, as shown in Figure 4-10.

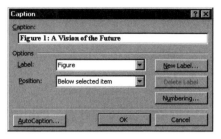

FIGURE 4-10

A caption in the Caption dialog box.

3 Type your caption in the Caption box. (Normally, you place a period or a colon between the number and the text of the caption.)

4 If necessary, select the type of item you are captioning from the Label drop-down list box.

5 Use the Position box to tell Word whether you want the caption above or below the item.

6 Click OK.

 If the type of item you want to caption isn't in the Label list, click New Label and enter it in the New Label dialog box. To change the numbering format for captions, click Numbering and select a different format from the Format drop-down list.

Using Mail Merge

If you want to mail letters (such as holiday greeting cards, announce-ments, or advertisements) to several people, you can use Word's Mail Merge Helper feature. You can combine a data list (names, addresses, and the like) with a Word document to print envelopes, mailing labels, and form letters. Here are the general steps:

1 Create a data list, called a **data source** in Word.

2 Create a main document that refers to the information in the data source.

3 Merge the main document with the data source to create person-alized letters, labels, or other documents.

Creating a Data Source

To create a data source, follow these steps:

1 Open a new blank document.

2 Choose the Tools menu's Mail Merge command to display the Mail Merge Helper dialog box, as shown in Figure 4-11.

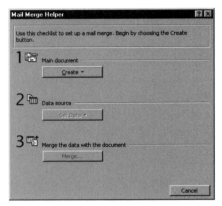

FIGURE 4-11

Use the Mail Merge Helper to set up a mail merge.

3 Click Create, and select the type of document you'll be creating. In this example, I've used Form Letters.

4 Word now asks if you want to create the document in the active **document window** or in a new document window. Click Active Window, since you've opened a new blank document.

5 Click Get Data, and select Create Data Source to display the Create Data Source dialog box, as shown in Figure 4-12.

FIGURE 4-12

The Create Data Source dialog box.

6 Scroll the list in the Field Names In Header Row box, and remove any field names you won't be using. In this example, I removed all but Title, FirstName, LastName, Address1, City, State, and PostalCode.

7 Click OK, and save the data source **file** you are about to create.

8 Next, you need to enter information in your data source, so click Edit Data Source to display the Data Form dialog box, as shown in Figure 4-13.

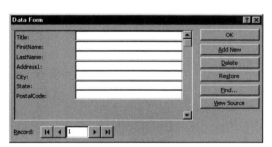

FIGURE 4-13

Complete a data form for each item in your data source.

9 For each person in your data source, complete a data form, entering their title, first name, last name, and so on in the appropriate field. When you've entered all the data for a person, click Add New to clear the form and enter the next person's data. When you've entered all the data for each person, click OK.

Creating the Main Document

Word now displays a blank screen on which you can create the main document and displays the Mail Merge toolbar just beneath the Personal toolbar. Figure 4-14 shows a document created using the Mail Merge toolbar. To enter the fields selected earlier in the Create Data Source dialog box, type the date (if you're creating a letter), press the Enter key a couple of times, and then click the Insert Merge Field toolbar button and select FirstName. Next, press the Spacebar, click the Insert Merge Field toolbar button, and select LastName. As you can see, Word places the field names within double angle brackets.

Be sure to press the Spacebar between fields such as FirstName and LastName. If you don't, the first and last names will appear as all one word in your printed letter.

FIGURE 4-14

The main document for a mail merge.

When you've finished typing your document and inserting the fields, click the View Merged Data toolbar button to preview your document. (This button appears on the Mail Merge toolbar, which Word adds to the program window after you choose the Tools menu's Mail Merge command.) To return to the main document, click the View Merged Data toolbar button again.

Merging Your Data Source and the Main Document

Now, if you're feeling brave and the preview looked okay, you can simply click the Merge To Printer button on the Mail Merge toolbar, and all your documents will start to print. A more cautious approach is to click the Merge To New Document toolbar button. Word does the merge and displays the results in a new document. You can then review the document before sending it to the printer.

You don't need to save the merge results. If you ever want to print the documents again, simply do the merge again.

One other option is to click the Merge toolbar button to display the Merge dialog box. You can use this dialog box to merge to e-mail or fax and to specify that only some records are to be merged. When you're finished, click Merge to merge the data source and the main document.

Follow these same basic steps to create mailing labels or envelopes.

Working with Special Document Elements

If you frequently create multipage documents, you might want to make use of Word's Headers and Footers feature to label the pages of your documents. If you produce reports and scholarly papers, you'll most certainly want to become familiar with how to insert footnotes and endnotes in a document. Another special document element is the cross-reference. You'll find cross-references scattered throughout this book and in many other publications, especially reference works. A cross-reference simply points you to another place in a document that has more or supplementary information about the topic under discussion.

Headers and Footers

If you want to insert text in the top or bottom margins of a document's pages, you use Word's Headers and Footers feature. The most common use of headers and footers is for page numbers (described in Chapter 3), but you can also add other elements to headers and footers, such as the name of the document, the date the document was last changed, or an **AutoText** entry.

 You can also use the header and footer areas to create a simple letterhead design for a document. For example, you can add your contact information in the bottom margin of your résumé.

To add header or footer text to your document, follow these steps:

1 Choose the View menu's Header And Footer command. Word places the insertion point in the header and displays the Header And Footer toolbar, as shown in Figure 4-15.

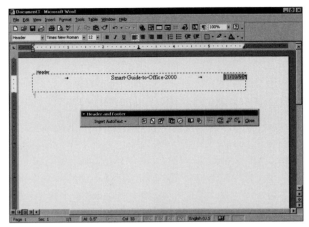

FIGURE 4-15

The Header box and the Header And Footer toolbar.

2 Enter the header text in the Header box. To enter page number elements, the date, the time, or an AutoText entry, you can use the Header And Footer toolbar's buttons.

 Notes *If you press the Tab key once and begin typing, Word centers the text across the page. If you press the Tab key once more and begin typing, Word aligns the text on the right side of the page.*

3 To enter a footer, click the Switch Between Header And Footer toolbar button and enter the footer text in the Footer box.

4 When you're finished entering the header and footer, click the Header And Footer toolbar's Close button.

 Notes *To allow different headers and footers on odd and even pages, click the Page Setup button on the Header And Footer toolbar and select the Different Odd And Even check box. To allow a different header on the first page (as in the case of letterhead), select the Different First Page check box. If you select either of these boxes, you can use the Header And Footer toolbar's Show Next and Show Previous buttons to display the second header or footer.*

Footnotes and Endnotes

One of the first features added to early **word processors** was the ability to insert notes at the bottom of the page or at the end of a document and to number them automatically. Anyone who went to high school, college, or graduate school back when I did (and I'm not saying exactly when that was) considers this feature a national treasure. On the other hand, those of you who came of age in the computer era probably will take this feature for granted, as you should.

By default, Word places footnotes at the bottom of the page and places endnotes at the end of the document. Footnotes have arabic numerals, and endnotes are numbered with lowercase roman numerals. You can customize this though, as you'll see shortly.

To insert a footnote or endnote, follow these steps:

1   Place the insertion point in the document where you want to insert the footnote or endnote.

2   Choose the Insert menu's Footnote command to display the Footnote And Endnote dialog box, as shown in Figure 4-16.

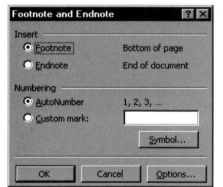

FIGURE 4-16

The Footnote And Endnote dialog box.

3   In the Insert section, click the option button for the type of note you want to insert.

4   In the Numbering section, accept Word's AutoNumber option, or click the Custom Mark option button and type your own footnote or endnote, or click Symbol to specify a symbol to use rather than a number or letter.

 Chapter 3 describes how to insert symbols.

5 To specify additional options, click Options to display the Note Options dialog box, which you can use to specify that notes start renumbering on each page or that the first note is numbered something other than 1.

6 You can also use the Note Options dialog box to convert all footnotes to endnotes and vice versa. Click Convert to display the Convert Notes dialog box.

7 When you have specified all your options, click OK to open a Footnote pane at the bottom of the screen, as shown in Figure 4-17.

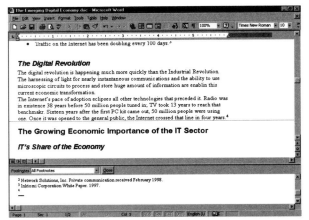

FIGURE 4-17

Enter footnote or endnote text in the pane at the bottom of the screen.

8 Following the number that Word inserts for you, enter the text of your note.

9 When you're finished, click Close to return to your document.

To read a footnote or an endnote, place the mouse pointer on the note number in the document. Word displays the note in a box, as shown in Figure 4-18.

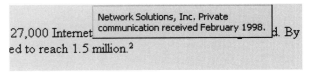

FIGURE 4-18

You can view a note in a pop-up box.

You can edit a note in Normal view or in Print Layout view. In Normal view, double-click the note number in the text to open the Footnote or Endnote pane at the bottom of the screen. Edit the text as you would edit any text. In Print Layout view, scroll to the bottom of the page to find the note, and then edit it as usual.

 I find editing a note in Normal view easier. In Normal view, you can simply toggle back and forth from the document to the notes pane and avoid all the scrolling.

To delete a note, select its number or symbol, and press the Delete key. All the remaining notes are automatically renumbered as necessary.

Cross–References

Using cross-references, you can point readers to a specific page or section heading (if it has been assigned a **style**) that is related to the current discussion. Word even verifies the accuracy of your cross-reference by checking to see that the page number or heading really exists and notifies you of any errors.

To insert a cross-reference to a section heading, follow these steps:

1 Enter the cross-reference text in your document, followed by a space and an opening quotation mark. Here's an example: *For more information on inserting footnotes or endnotes in a document, see ".*

2 Choose the Insert menu's Cross-Reference command to display the Cross-Reference dialog box, as shown in Figure 4-19.

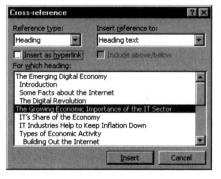

FIGURE 4-19

Inserting a cross-reference to a section heading.

3 Select Heading from the Reference Type drop-down list box. All the headings in your document are displayed in the For Which Heading list box.

4 Select the heading to which you want to cross-reference, and click Insert.

5 Word inserts the heading in your document immediately after the quotation mark you entered.

6 Click Close to close the Cross-Reference dialog box.

7 Back in your document, enter a period and closing quotation mark.

Before you can cross-reference a page number, you need to **bookmark** it. To do this, follow these steps:

1 Place the insertion point in a paragraph on the page to which you want to cross-reference.

2 Choose the Insert menu's Bookmark command to display the Bookmark dialog box, as shown in Figure 4-20.

FIGURE 4-20

Inserting a bookmark.

3 In the Bookmark Name text box, type a name (with no spaces) for the bookmark, for example, Page20, and click Add.

4 Back in your document, type the cross-reference text. Here's an example: *For more information on inserting footnotes and endnotes in your document, see page* . (Enter a space after the word *page*.)

5 Choose the Insert menu's Cross-Reference command to display the Cross-Reference dialog box.

6 Select Bookmark from the Reference Type drop-down list box, and select the bookmark name from the For Which Bookmark list.

7 Select Page Number from the Insert Reference To drop-down list box.

8 Click Insert, and the page number appears in your document following the word *page.*

9 Click Close to close the Cross-Reference dialog box.

10 Type a period following the page number you inserted in the document.

 For more information about bookmarks, choose the Help menu's Microsoft Word Help command, click the Index tab, and search on bookmark.

CHAPTER 5

Excel Basics

Even if you don't consider yourself a "numbers" person, you'll find many useful applications for **Microsoft Excel 2000.** You can use it for budgeting, forecasting, and quantitative analysis of just about any kind of data. In addition, Excel also provides other tools you can use to better understand your data, including a powerful **Chart Wizard** that lets you easily create graphs. This chapter describes the following tasks:

- Creating a blank **workbook**
- Filling workbooks with data
- Building **formulas**
- Moving and **copying** workbook **ranges**
- Formatting cells
- Making charts

Creating a Blank Workbook

Excel opens a blank workbook **document** whenever you start the program. Figure 5-1 shows the Excel **program window** with a blank workbook. Excel initially names the workbook Book1. You change the workbook's name when you save it. As described in Chapter 1, you save a workbook using the File **menu's** Save As command.

 As noted in Chapter 1, a workbook is just a grid, or **spreadsheet,** of boxes you can use to organize your data.

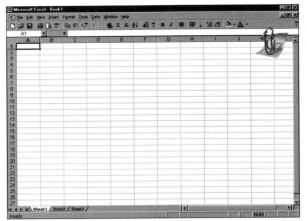

FIGURE 5-1

The Excel program window with a blank workbook.

You can open additional blank workbooks by **clicking** the New Workbook **toolbar** button. As you open additional workbook documents, Excel names them Book2, Book3, Book4, and so on.

You can also create blank documents by choosing the File menu's New command. When you choose this command, Excel displays the New Workbook **dialog box**, as shown in Figure 5-2. The New Workbook dialog box provides tabs, which list workbook templates you can use as the basis for building a new workbook. The General tab, for example, lists the blank document Excel uses when it starts and when you click the New Workbook toolbar button. Other tabs list other, partially complete workbook documents that you can use. By using one of these **document templates**, you often save time.

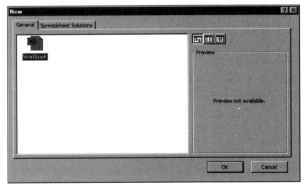

FIGURE 5-2

The New Workbook dialog box.

Filling Workbooks with Data

You build your workbooks by entering data into the **cells** of the workbook. The cells of the workbook are input boxes, or blanks, that you fill in. Excel arranges the cells of the workbook into rows and columns, numbering the rows to uniquely identify them and assigning letters to the columns to uniquely identify them.

 Notes

Excel's workbooks provide 65,536 rows and 256 columns. Rows, as noted earlier, are numbered 1, 2, 3, and so on all the way to 65,536. Columns are labeled A, B, C, and so on all the way to column Z. The next set of columns is labeled AA, AB, AC, and so on all the way to AZ. Then, the next set of columns is labeled BA, BB, BC, and so on.

You can enter two types of data into a cell: **labels** and **values**. A label is typically a block of text, although a label can use numbers and symbols. The distinguishing characteristic of a label is that it won't later be used in a formula. In other words, you don't use labels in mathematical calculations. In Figure 5-3, the cells in column A hold labels.

A value typically is a number you want to use in a calculation. In the workbook shown in Figure 5-3, for example, column C holds values. Cell C1 holds the value 2500, for example. And cell C2 holds the value 3500. The distinguishing feature of a value is that a value can be used in a formula.

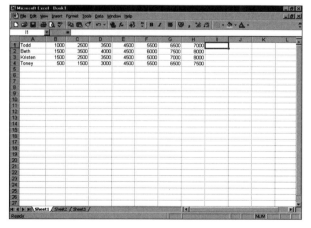

FIGURE 5-3

An Excel workbook with a handful of labels and values stored in cells.

Notes *Formulas represent a special type of value, as described in the later section "Building Formulas."*

To enter a label or value into a cell, follow these steps:

1 Click the cell into which you want to enter a label or value. Excel marks the cell with a dark border, called a **cell selector.** The cell selector identifies the cell you will fill with data.

Notes *You don't have to click the mouse to move the cell selector to the cell you want to fill with data. You can also press the arrow keys.*

2 Type the label or value you want to enter. For all practical purposes, you can enter labels of any length and values of any size.

3 If a cell isn't initially wide enough to display your label or value, you can increase the column width in two easy ways: You can point to the border, or line, between the two column letter buttons; then, when the mouse pointer turns into a double-sided arrow, double-click the border. (This tells Excel to expand the column width to just slightly larger than the widest entry.) Or you can point to the border, or line, between the two column letter buttons; then, when the mouse pointer turns into a double-sided arrow, drag the border to resize the column.

4 Press the Enter key or one of the arrow keys to indicate that you've finished your entry. If you press the Enter key, Excel moves the cell selector to the next lower cell. If you press an arrow key, Excel moves the cell selector in the direction of the arrow.

Let me mention a few additional points about entering values into a cell. First, although you can enter values into cells using just the number keys and, if necessary, the period key to represent the decimal place, you can also include formatting characters in your entry. If you use characters such as currency symbols and commas in your entry, Excel uses these symbols to format the displayed number. Note, however, that the symbols aren't actually part of the value. They're just formatting used to display the value. I talk more about formatting workbook values in the later section "Formatting Cells."

Second, Excel considers anything that looks like a time or date to be a value. Excel does this so you can build date-based and time-based arithmetic. I talk more about date and time formulas in the next section, "Building Formulas."

Third, Excel can automatically enter data in a cell if it can follow the simple addition or subtraction pattern you're creating. For example, if you enter 5 in one cell and 10 in the next cell, Excel assumes you're adding 5 to each additional cell in the row or column. Select the first two cells and drag the handle in the lower right corner of the range to have Excel continue the pattern down the column or across the row. Likewise, if you enter January in one cell and drag the handle in the lower right corner of the cell, Excel continues filling in the names of the months in the cells you drag across.

Finally, Excel lets you use scientific notation to enter especially large or especially small values. Scientific notation, as you may know, expresses values as numbers raised to a power of 10. For example, the value 1,525,000 can be expressed using the scientific notation:

$$1.525 \times 10^6$$

Because 10^6 equals 1,000,000, this notation is a shorthand way of saying the value is $1.525 \times 1,000,000$, which equals 1,525,000.

Similarly, the value .0000001234 can be expressed using the scientific notation:

$$1.234 \times 10^{-7}$$

Because 10^{-7} equals .0000001, this notation is a shorthand way of saying the value is $1.234 \times .0000001$, which equals .0000001234.

Figure 5-4 shows how Excel expresses scientific notation. Notice that Excel replaces the × 10 portion of a scientific notation with an E. In addition, the power isn't shown as a superscript.

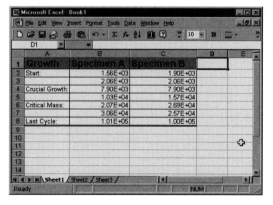

FIGURE 5-4

An Excel workbook with values displayed using scientific notation.

Notes *If you enter a value that's very large or very small, Excel might display the value using scientific notation and, in some cases, might even convert the value to scientific notation.*

Building Formulas

The ability to organize your data into rows and columns makes Excel useful, of course, but this feature isn't all that compelling. However, Excel also lets you build formulas that use the values you've stored in a worksheet. And this ability to build and use formulas is what gives Excel its real power. Therefore, I'm going to spend the largest portion of this chapter discussing in detail how you work with Excel's formulas.

Formula Basics

Excel lets you enter formulas into workbook cells. Excel stores the formula in the cell but displays the formula result onscreen and in printed workbooks.

To build a formula, follow these steps:

1 Click the cell into which you want to enter the formula. Excel marks the cell with a dark border, called a cell selector. The cell selector identifies the cell you will fill with data.

2 Type the equals sign (=) to tell Excel you're about to enter a formula.

3 Type the formula you want to have calculated using the appropriate values and **operators.** Use the plus sign (+) for addition, the minus sign (-) for subtraction, the asterisk symbol (*) for multiplication, and the slash symbol (/) for division.

4 Press the Enter key. Excel calculates the formula and displays the result onscreen, as shown in Figure 5-5.

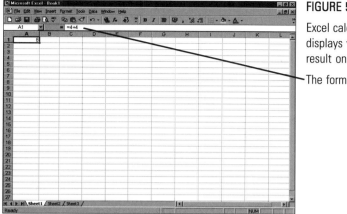

FIGURE 5-5

Excel calculates and then displays your formula's result onscreen.

The formula appears here.

To edit an existing formula, follow these steps:

1 Double-click the cell with the formula. Excel opens a text box over the cell.

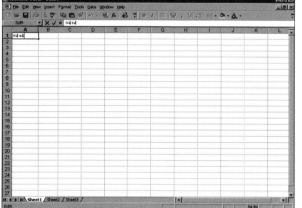

FIGURE 5-6

When you double-click a cell, Excel displays the cell's formula in an editable text box.

2 Edit the formula by replacing or erasing operators and operands.

3 When you finish, press the Enter key. Excel recalculates the formula and displays the result onscreen, as shown in Figure 5-6.

Table 5-1 shows some more sample formulas. Take a moment to look through them.

Formula	Formula Description and Result
=1+2	Adds 1 and 2 returning a result of 3.
=3-4	Subtracts 4 from 3 returning a result of -1.
=5*6	Multiplies 5 by 6 returning a result of 30.
=7/8	Divides 7 by 8 returning a result of .875.

TABLE 5-1: Sample formulas.

Using Cell References in Formulas

While you can build formulas using values, you can also use **cell references** in formulas. For example, if you enter the value 2 into both cells A1 and B1, the following formula returns the value 4 because 2 plus 2 equals 4:

=A1+B1

You can also combine values and cell references in a formula, too. For example, if you enter the value 2 into both cells A1 and B1, the following formula returns the value 8 because 2 plus 2 plus 4 equals 8:

=A1+B1+4

 Notes *If you build a formula that Excel recognizes as erroneous, Excel displays an error message rather than trying to display some formula result. For example, if you enter the formula =1/0 into a cell, Excel returns the error message #DIV/0!.*

Using cell references in formulas makes your workbooks more flexible. Figure 5-7, for example, shows a simple budgeting worksheet. Cell B5 calculates the total expenses budgeted using the following formula:

=B2+B3+B4

The preceding formula simply adds the values stored in cells B2, B3, and B4.

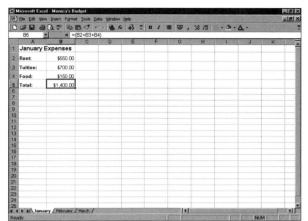

FIGURE 5-7

In this workbook, the formula in cell B5 uses cell references.

 When entering cell references into a formula, you can click the cell you want to reference instead of typing its address.

One big advantage of using cell references in formulas is that Excel recalculates the formula any time a precedent cell's value changes. For example, if you constructed a workbook like the one shown in Figure 5-7 and then changed the value in cell B2, Excel would automatically calculate the formula in cell B5.

Working with Special Operators

Most of the formulas you build will use only the standard arithmetic operators for addition, subtraction, multiplication, and division. Excel, however, supplies several more esoteric operators. You can use the ^ symbol, for example, for exponential operations. You can use comparison operators like the greater-than symbol (>) and the less-than symbol (<) for comparison operations.

The exponential operator lets you raise a value to some power. For example, if you want to square the value 12—which is the same thing as raising 12 to the second power—you can use the following formula:

$$=12^2$$

If you want to cube the value 4—which is the same thing as raising 4 to the third power—you can use the following formula:

=4^3

When you use a comparison operator, Excel compares two values. If the two values pass the logical test, the formula returns TRUE. If the two values don't pass the logical test, the formula returns FALSE. If you aren't used to working with comparison operators, this can be confusing. Table 5-2 shows some example comparison formulas.

Formula	Formula Description and Result
=1=1	Compares the value 1 to the value 1 using the equals operator (=) to see if they are equal. Because these two values are equal, the formula returns TRUE.
=2<>2	Compares the value 2 to the value 2 using the not-equal operator (<>) to see if they are not equal. Because these two values are equal, the formula returns FALSE.
=3<4	Compares the value 3 to the value 4 using the less-than operator (<) to see if 3 is less than 4. Because 3 is less than 4, the formula returns TRUE.
=5>6	Compares the value 5 to the value 6 using the greater-than operator (>) to see if 5 is greater than 6. Because 5 is not greater than 6, the formula returns FALSE.
=7<=8	Compares the value 7 to the value 8 using the less-than-or-equal-to operator (<=) to see if 7 is less than or equal to 8. Because 7 is less than 8, the formula returns TRUE.
=9>=10	Compares the value 9 to the value 10 using the greater-than-or-equal-to operator (>=) to see if 9 is greater than or equal to 10. Because 9 is less than 10, the formula returns FALSE.

TABLE 5-2: Comparison formulas.

Notes *The TRUE result that a comparison operator returns actually equals the value 1. The FALSE result that a comparison operator returns actually equals 0.*

Notes | *Excel also lets you include text strings in formulas using the concatenation operator (&). For example, if a workbook contains a column of first names and a column of last names, you could combine the names in a third column. To combine a first name in cell A1 with a space and the last name in cell B1, you would enter the formula =A1&" "&B1. Or if you had a budget based on an inflation rate listed in cell A1, you could create a label cell that noted this fact by entering ="This budget is based on an inflation rate of "&A1. Note that quotation marks are used around the text included in the formulas in these examples. When entering text in a formula, always put it in quotation marks.*

Understanding Operator Precedence

You can build a single formula that uses several operators. When a formula uses multiple operators, Excel applies the standard rules of operator precedence:

- Exponential operators are performed first.
- Multiplication and division operators are performed second.
- Addition and subtraction operators are performed third.
- Comparison operators are performed fourth.

5

If you want to override the standard rules of operator precedence, you use parentheses. Enclose the first operation—both the operator and the operands—that you want calculated inside parentheses. Then, enclose the second operation inside parentheses, and so on.

This business about operator precedence and how you override the standard precedence can be confusing if you haven't done much arithmetic lately. Table 5-3 shows and describes several simple formulas.

Formula	Description and Result
=1+2*3	Multiplies 2 times 3 and then adds 1, returning the value 7.
=(1+2)*3	Adds 1 plus 2, then multiplies this result (3) by 3, returning the value 9.
=1+2^3	Raises the value 2 to the third power and then adds 1, returning the value 9.
=(1+2)^3	Adds 1 plus 2, then raises this result to the third power, returning the value 27.

TABLE 5-3: Simple formulas.

Date and Time Formulas

Excel considers anything that looks like a date or time to be a value, using the integer portion of a value to represent the date and the decimal portion of a value to represent the time. Date and time values sound complicated at first—and perhaps a bit strange. But by treating dates and times as values, you can easily perform date-based and time-based arithmetic.

For example, if you want to calculate the due date of an invoice that's supposed to be paid 45 days from January 13, 2000, you can easily do so with a date formula. All you do is add 45 to the date value for January 13, 2000.

 Notes *Excel uses the value 0 to represent January 1, 1900, the value 1 to represent January 2, 1900, and so on, all the way to the value 2,958,465 to represent December 31, 9999.*

Figure 5-8 shows an example of this calculation. Cell B1 shows January 13, 2000. Excel sees that this is a date and so actually stores the date value for this date in cell B1. The date value for January 13, 2000, is 36,538. Cell B2 holds the value 45. Cell B3 holds a formula =B1+B2, which adds the date value 36,538 to 45, returning the date value 36,583. Note that Excel formats the values shown in cells B1 and B3 to show as dates.

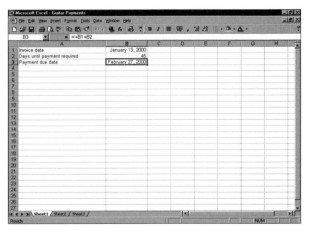

FIGURE 5-8

This workbook uses some simple date-based arithmetic.

Excel uses four-digit year numbers—and always has—so you shouldn't need to worry about the "Year 2000" issue. Note, however, that because Excel does use four-digit year numbers, dates that fall after December 31, 9999, could pose a "Year 10,000" problem.

You can use Excel to perform time-based arithmetic as well. For example, if you want to calculate the minutes worked by someone who started at 8:12 AM, took a 24-minute lunch, and then stopped work at 4:32 PM, you can easily do so with a time formula. Figure 5-9 shows a simple workbook that makes this calculation.

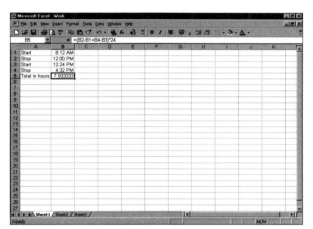

FIGURE 5-9

This workbook uses some simple time-based arithmetic.

Cells B1, B2, B3, and B4 hold the time values that show the work start and stop times. Cell B5 holds a formula that calculates the total working time, as shown below:

=(B2-B1+B4-B3)*24

Here's what's happening with the formula. The *B2-B1* part of the formula calculates the fractional day worked in the morning. The *B4-B3* part of the formula calculates the fractional part of the day worked in the afternoon. Adding these two values together calculates the fraction, or percentage, of the day that's worked. This value, which happens to be roughly .3305555, is multiplied by the number of hours in a day, 24, to get the number of hours worked—in this case, 7.933333.

Using Function-Based Formulas

You can build many formulas by hand using the arithmetic operators. In the preceding pages of this chapter, in fact, I've shown you many simple formulas that you can build in just this manner. But you can't build every formula in this way. Many formulas are too complicated or lengthy to build by hand. You can't really build a formula that calculates loan payments by hand, for example. And you can't easily build a formula that needs to add 50 values using just the addition operator (+).

Fortunately, Excel provides formula building blocks called **functions.** Functions amount to prebuilt formulas. With a function, you supply the input values needed by the function. The function then manipulates the values in whatever manner necessary to make the calculation.

To use a function, you typically use the Paste Function dialog box, which lets you select the function you want to use in your calculation and then prompts you for the input values. To show you how this works, suppose that you want to calculate the total expenses budgeted in Figure 5-10, adding cells B2 through B13.

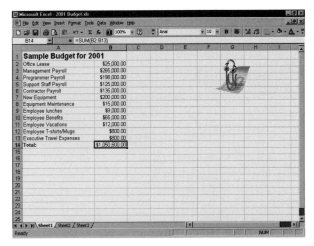

FIGURE 5-10

This workbook shows an example of budgeted expenses.

To use a function in a formula, you take seven steps:

1 Click cell B14.

2 Click the Paste Function toolbar button. Excel displays the first Paste Function dialog box, as shown in Figure 5-11.

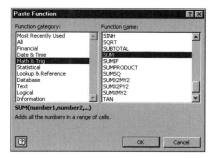

FIGURE 5-11

The first Paste Function dialog box.

3 Select the Math & Trig entry in the Function Category list. The Function Category list just identifies the major groupings of function categories. When you select an entry in the Function Category list, Excel uses the Function Name list to show the functions in that category.

 Excel provides a rich set of functions you can use in your formulas, including functions for making financial calculations, statistical calculations, and date and time functions. You'll want to explore those categories of functions that provide functions you might need in your workbook construction.

4 Select the function you want to use in the Function Name list. You might need to scroll through the Function Name list to find the function you want. When you select an entry in the Function Name list, Excel describes the function in the area beneath the list boxes.

5 Click OK. Excel displays the second Paste Function dialog box, as shown in Figure 5-12.

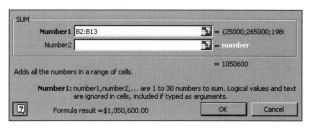

FIGURE 5-12

The second Paste Function dialog box.

6 Use the text boxes to identify the inputs you need for the function. In the case of the workbook shown in Figure 5-10, you would do this by entering *B2:B13* into the Number 1 text box. The entry B2:B13 tells Excel you want to use all the values in the range of cells from B2 to B13.

7 Click OK. Excel closes the Paste Function dialog box and places the function-based formula into the cell you selected in step 1. Figure 5-13 shows the workbook from Figure 5-10, only this time with a function-based formula in cell B14.

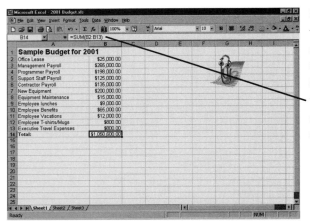

FIGURE 5-13

This workbook shows an example of budgeted expenses—this time summed to show the total.

The formula bar shows the contents of cell B14, a simple =SUM() function.

The function-based formula in cell B14 is

=SUM(B2:B13)

As shown in Figure 5-13, a function-based formula begins with the equals sign (=). Following the equals sign is the function name—SUM in Figure 5-13. And then following the function name, parentheses enclose the function's input values.

---

*Excel actually provides an **AutoSum** toolbar button you can use to enter =SUM functions into cells. In the case of the workbook shown in Figures 5-10 and 5-13, you could also enter the =SUM formula into cell B14 by selecting the workbook range B2:B14 and then clicking the AutoSum button. To select a workbook range, click the first cell in the range—B2 in this example—and then drag the mouse to the last cell in the range—B14 in this example. The AutoSum toolbar button is the one that shows a summation symbol.*

You now know much of what you need to know to use functions in formulas. Even so, I want to quickly provide you with several additional pieces of useful information.

If a function requires multiple **arguments,** or input values, you separate the arguments with commas. For example, to calculate a loan payment that charges a 1% per month interest rate, requires payments over 120 months, and is for a $100,000 loan, you must provide the loan payment function, PMT, with three arguments, as shown below:

=PMT(0.01,120,100000)

Note, too, that you can use values, cell references, and even formulas as function arguments, which means that both of the following loan payment functions are equivalent to the preceding loan function as long as cells B1, B2, and B3 hold the values 0.01, 120, and 100000:

=PMT(B1,B2,B3)

=PMT(B1,12*10,B3)

 Excel requires function arguments to be entered in exactly the right order, but the Paste Function dialog boxes will show you the order.

One other point to make is that some functions don't require arguments. For example, Excel provides a function for returning the mathematical value for pi, 3.14159265358979. If you want to use pi in some workbook, however, you use the following function:

=PI()

---

 *Often an easy way to find a function is to use the **Office Assistant,** as described in Chapter 1. You can ask the Office Assistant a question, such as "How do I calculate a loan payment?" When you do this, the Office Assistant creates a list of functions that might work for your purpose.*

Moving and Copying Workbook Ranges

You can build a workbook by filling it one cell at a time. Excel also lets you move and copy workbook ranges, however, making workbook construction easier and faster.

What Is a Range?

A range is any rectangle of cells. The smallest range, therefore, is a single cell. The largest range is an entire worksheet. Figure 5-14 shows several range examples.

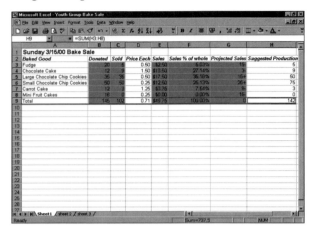

FIGURE 5-14

This workbook shows several range selections.

If you've selected a range, Excel highlights the active cell into which any data is placed.

 Notes *Excel also lets you work with three-dimensional ranges, or **cubes**. Although this book doesn't discuss three-dimensional ranges in detail, you generally work with them in the same way that you work with two-dimensional ranges.*

Selecting a Range

To select a range, you can use either the mouse or the keyboard, but most people find the mouse easiest. To select a workbook range with the mouse, follow these steps:

1 Click one of the range's corner cells. In Figure 5-15, you could click cell B2 since it is a corner cell of the selected range.

2 Drag the mouse to the opposite corner's cell. In Figure 5-15, you would drag the mouse to cell E8 if you clicked cell B2 in step 1.

 Notes *If you want to extend the range to other worksheets, hold down the Ctrl key and click the other worksheets' tabs. If you do this, by the way, you actually select a three-dimensional range, or cube.*

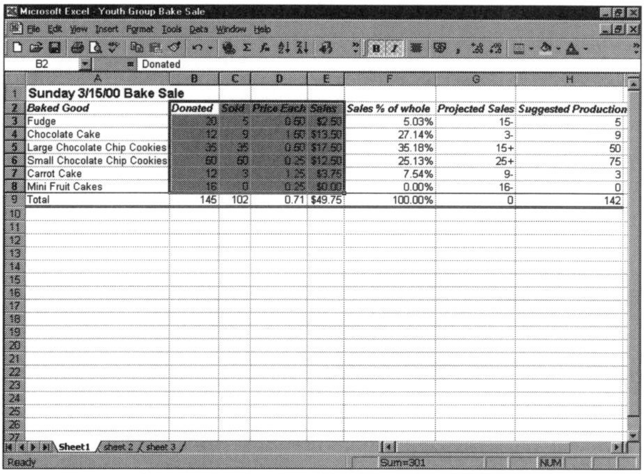

FIGURE 5-15

In this workbook, the range B2:E8 is selected.

You can also select a workbook range with the keyboard. To select a workbook range with the keyboard, follow these steps:

1. Use the arrow keys to make one of the range's corner cells the active cell. In Figure 5-15, you could use the arrow keys to select cell B2 since it is a corner cell of the selected range.
2. Press and hold down the Shift key.
3. Use the arrow keys to extend the range. In Figure 5-15, you could press the Right arrow key three times and the Down arrow key six times to select the range B2:E8 if you made cell B2 active in step 1.

5

Moving and Copying a Range

If you want to relocate workbook data—values, labels, and formulas—you do so by moving the range. If you want to duplicate the data stored in the workbook, you do so by copying the range. You can move or copy a range by using either the mouse or menu commands.

To move or copy a range with the mouse, simply follow these steps:

1. Select the range using the mouse.
2. Point to the range selection's border so the mouse pointer changes to an arrow.
3. Drag the selection to its new location. If you want to copy the range, hold down the Ctrl key as you do so. As you drag the mouse, Excel shows where you're moving the range by drawing a gray border around the range into which you'll move the selected range when you release the mouse button (see Figure 5-16). Excel also displays the range name with a small label.

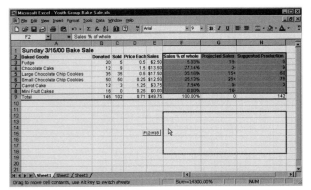

FIGURE 5-16

Excel shows you where you've dragged a range selection using a gray border and a small label.

To move a range with the **Cut** and **Paste** commands, follow these steps:

1 Select the range using the keyboard or mouse.

2 Choose the Edit menu's Cut command. Or click the Cut toolbar button.

3 Use the arrow keys to select the top left corner of the range into which you want to place the cut range.

4 Choose the Edit menu's Paste command. Or click the Paste toolbar button. Excel moves the range to its new location.

When you move or copy data to a new workbook location, you remove any data already residing there.

*Remember that you can use the **Clipboard** toolbar to work with multiple selections, as described in Chapter 2 in the section "Copying Text."*

Moving and Copying Formulas

You can move and copy formulas, as you've probably guessed. What you may not have guessed, however, is that Excel is very smart about the way it adjusts formulas when they are moved.

Let's begin with the way Excel adjusts formulas when you move workbook data. To make this as simple as possible, look at the workbook shown in Figure 5-17, and note that the formula in cell B4 adds the total expenses using the formula =B1+B2+B3.

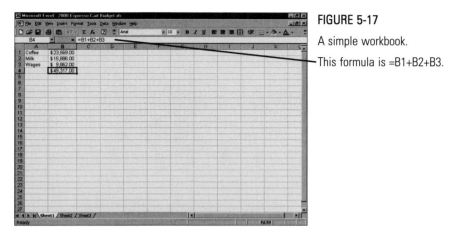

FIGURE 5-17

A simple workbook.

This formula is =B1+B2+B3.

In the case of the workbook shown in Figure 5-17, Excel adjusts the formula in cell B4 if you move any of the contents of any of the cells referenced by the formula. If you move the contents of cell B1 to cell C1, for example, Excel adjusts the formula in cell B4 to read =C1+B2+B3, as shown in Figure 5-18.

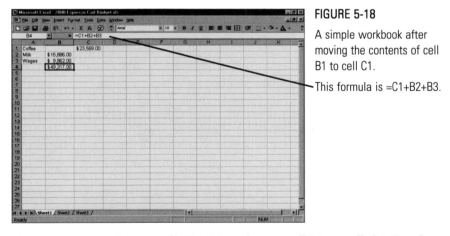

FIGURE 5-18

A simple workbook after moving the contents of cell B1 to cell C1.

This formula is =C1+B2+B3.

If you enter new data in cells C1:C3 and copy cell B4 to cell C4, Excel inserts the formula from cell B4. When Excel places the formula into cell C4, it rewrites the formula as =C1+C2+C3, as shown in Figure 5-19. In other words, it considers the cell references used in a copied formula to be relative.

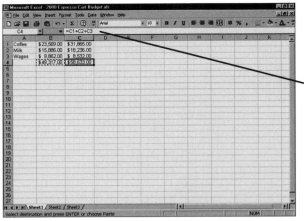

FIGURE 5-19

A simple workbook after copying the formula from cell B4 to cell C4.

This formula is =C1+C2+C3.

Formatting Cells

Excel allows you to control the way numbers and text are displayed. This formatting saves you time, greatly improves the appearance of your workbooks, and makes them more legible for presentations. This section discusses how to format numbers and use the AutoFormat tool in Excel.

Formatting Numbers

You can use the Format menu's Cells command to specify how values in a selected range should be displayed. For example, you can tell Excel to use currency symbols for values representing dollars, Deutsche mark, or yen. And you can tell Excel to use symbols such as commas and percentages to make values easier to read. To make these sorts of changes, follow these steps:

1   Select the range containing the numbers you want to format.

2   Choose the Format menu's Cells command to display the Format Cells dialog box. It contains six tabs used to format cells. In this example, we discuss the Number tab, as shown in Figure 5-20.

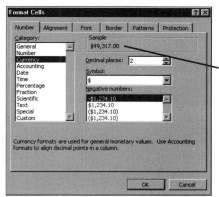

FIGURE 5-20

The Format Cells dialog box with the Number tab displayed.

When you select a category, the Sample box shows you how that number will look.

3 Select a category of formatting choices from the Category list box. Excel displays the choices for that category. Each category has a specific set of choices. When you select Currency, for example, you can specify how many places to carry out the decimal point, what currency symbol to use, and how to treat negative values.

4 Use the formatting choice buttons and boxes to specify how Excel should display the values in the selected range.

 Excel provides a rich set of formatting choices. The Special category includes Zip codes, Zip +4, phone numbers, and social security numbers. The Custom category has formats you can customize yourself. The General category is Excel's default setting, which accepts text or numbers.

AutoFormatting a Workbook Selection

You can choose from among many different predesigned worksheet formats in Excel. This saves you the time of going through and editing the worksheet to make it look appealing. You can either AutoFormat your worksheet before you start entering data or you can select a worksheet you have been working on and have Excel go through and reformat it in the new **style.**

To AutoFormat your workbook, follow these steps:

1 Select the worksheet range you want to format.

2 Choose the Format menu's AutoFormat command to display the AutoFormat dialog box. You can choose from 17 different styles in the AutoFormat dialog box by scrolling through them. (Most of the examples use a representation of a calendar to give you an idea of how the formatting will look.)

3 Click OK. Excel changes the format of the selected cells to match the displayed example, as shown in Figure 5-21.

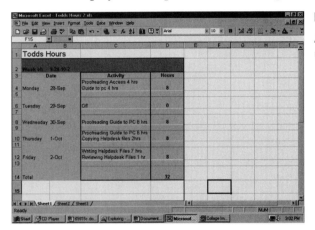

FIGURE 5-21

A spreadsheet formatted using the AutoFormat tool.

Making Charts

Excel allows you to graphically display all types of information in charts. You can display anything from a large corporation's profits and losses to a graphical illustration of who ate the largest piece of pie at dinner. This section discusses the different types of charts, how to set up your Excel data to make a chart, how to use the Chart Wizard, and how to copy your charts into other Office **programs.**

Types of Charts

Quantitative information can be shown on 14 different types of charts in Excel. As long as you have two numbers, you can make a chart to compare them. Pie charts, bar graphs, line graphs, and three-dimensional charts are examples of the charts available in the Chart Wizard.

Figure 5-22 shows an example of different types of charts you can create using the same set of numbers.

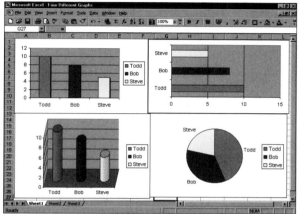

FIGURE 5-22

Four different Excel charts that use the same data but present it differently.

Data Series and Data Categories

Excel does all the work of making pictures out of numbers for you; however, you still have to come up with the numbers. And since charts are all about comparing numbers, let's talk about the two different types of relationships numbers can have on a chart.

The two different types of data you can put into a chart are called **data series** and data categories. Data series provide the values you plot in a chart: interest rates, wages, or sales. Data categories organize and order the values in a data series. Let's look at a couple of charts to illustrate these data types.

 In any chart that shows how something changes over time, the time intervals are the data category.

Figure 5-23 shows a chart that illustrates a company's projected sales over the next 10 years. The data series is a set of sales estimates, and the data category is time.

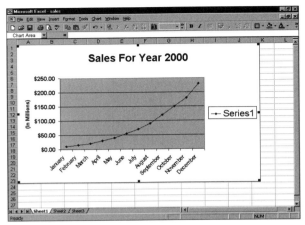

FIGURE 5-23

An Excel chart showing a data series of sales in which the data category is time.

 You can often use a simple trick to identify a chart's data series. Ask yourself the question, "What does this chart show?" Every one-word answer is a data series.

Figure 5-24 also shows the data series projected sales; however, in this case the data category is different people.

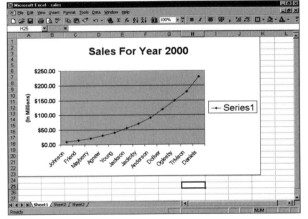

FIGURE 5-24

An Excel chart showing a data series of sales in which the data category is different people.

Often when you think, "I'll show this information on a chart," you have an idea of what information you will be comparing and how you might compare it. However, it's good to know the difference between data series and data categories so you can decide which type of chart will best display your information. For example, pie charts look great visually, but they can display only one data series, while bar and line charts can display multiple series of data on a given data category. Radar and scatter charts can show multiple data series and categories, but it's easy to get the categories confused.

Gathering Your Data

Before you make a chart, you must collect your data. Excel lets you enter your data horizontally in rows or vertically in columns in a workbook. However, you can enter data into only 256 columns before your worksheet ends. So if you've got more data points than that, you'll need to enter your data series in rows. (Excel has 65,536 rows.)

Figure 5-25 shows a data series all lined up, selected, and ready to go. By including a title for each column of numbers, the Chart Wizard will identify to whom the data series belongs.

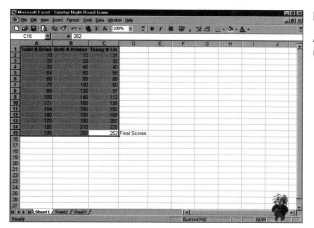

FIGURE 5-25

A data series ready for the Chart Wizard.

It's important that you select the range of cells in which your data is included so the Chart Wizard knows which numbers to use. In Figure 5-25, I selected the cells A1:C15. To do this, click the top left corner of the cells that contain your data and then drag the mouse to the bottom right corner.

Using the Chart Wizard

The Chart Wizard guides you through a series of steps to make your chart. (Remember, before you start, you need to enter all your data into an Excel worksheet.)

You can go back and change the original data on the worksheet and Excel will automatically change the chart to reflect your changes.

To start the Chart Wizard, follow these steps:

1 Select the data for the Chart Wizard to use, if you haven't already done so.

2 Choose the Insert menu's Chart command to display the Chart Type dialog box, as shown in Figure 5-26. The dialog box displays the different chart options with a list of chart types on the left and sub-types on the right. For each chart type there are usually several sub-types. After you select the sub-type of chart you want to use, click Press And Hold To View Sample for a preview of how your data will look using the highlighted chart.

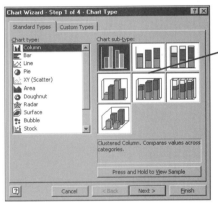

FIGURE 5-26

The first Chart Wizard dialog box.

Almost every chart type has a 3-D sub-type.

 The buttons listed along the bottom of the Chart Wizard dialog box allow you to navigate through the wizard. If you click Next, but decide you don't like the choice you made, click Back to go to the previous dialog box and change your selection.

3 Select a type from the Chart Type list box.

4 Select a sub-type from the Chart Sub-Type examples.

5 Click Next to display the Chart Source Data window, as shown in Figure 5-27. A preview of your chart, based on the data in your worksheet, shows the exact range of cells you selected in the Data Range text box. Assuming you chose the correct set of cells for your chart data, this is basically how the chart will look.

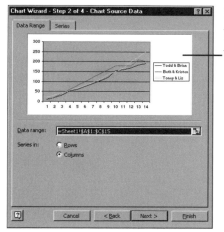

FIGURE 5-27

The second Chart Wizard dialog box.

This is a preview of your chart.

6 Click Next to proceed to the Chart Options dialog box, as shown in Figure 5-28. Excel lets you customize your chart with several options, including a title, **X-axis** name, **Y-axis** name, gridlines, **legend** placement, data labels, and **source data table.** After the chart is made, you can go in and modify elements such as **font,** color, letter placement, and other features. For now, select the options you want from the tabs in this dialog box. If you're in a hurry, just give the chart a title and click Next to proceed to the next dialog box.

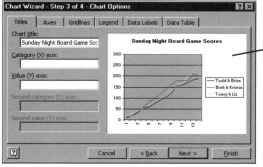

FIGURE 5-28

The Chart Options dialog box.

When you enter your options in the text boxes, Excel previews them for you.

7 Click Next to display the Chart Location dialog box, as shown in Figure 5-29. In this dialog box, tell Excel where you want the chart to go. In most cases, you will want it on the worksheet in which you entered your data, which is the default location. But if you would like it somewhere else, now is the time to say so.

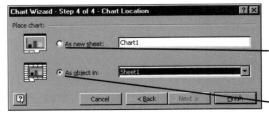

FIGURE 5-29

The Chart Location dialog box.

Clicking this option button tells Excel to put the chart on a completely new worksheet.

Clicking this option button allows you to specify a worksheet on which you would like the chart to be placed. (Or leave it on the default worksheet, which is the open one.)

 You can export Excel charts into other Office programs by simply copying the chart in Excel and pasting it in the other program. This is a great feature because, although other Office programs might have chart-making functions, Excel's Chart Wizard is by far the best and easiest to use.

8 Select a location for your chart, or ignore this screen to put the chart on your open worksheet.

9 Click Finish to create your chart.

When you finish the Chart Wizard, Excel places the chart on the worksheet, as shown in Figure 5-30.

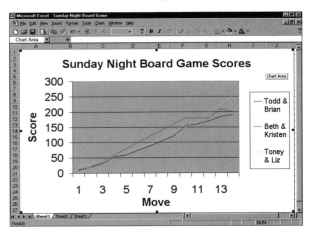

FIGURE 5-30

A completed chart created by the Chart Wizard.

You can print your chart the same way you print an Excel worksheet, as described in Chapter 2.

Formatting Your Chart

After Excel places your chart on the worksheet, you can easily customize the chart by moving it, changing its appearance, or making it fit your presentation. Here are some general instructions for doing this:

- To move the chart, click it and drag the chart to its new location.

- To move any of the parts of the chart to a different location, such as the legend, the title, or the axis labels, click the element and drag it to its new location.

- To make an element on your chart larger or smaller, select the element by clicking it and then place the mouse pointer over one of the selection handles on the side or corner of the element. Click a selection handle, and drag it to increase or decrease the size of the element.

- To change the format of any of your chart's elements, right-click the element and choose the shortcut menu's Format command. For example, you can change the color of your chart's data series, the font or size of the numbers, or the alignment of the text (see Figure 5-31).

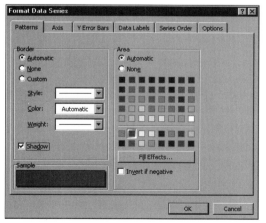

FIGURE 5-31

The Format Data Series dialog box.

To further customize your chart, select a color from the palette to change your chart's color scheme or select the Shadow check box to give the data series a shadow effect. Selecting a custom border highlights the borders of the data series differently. To change other properties of the data series, click the different tabs.

 To change the format of any of the written or numerical characters on your chart, right-click them, choose the shortcut menu's Format command, and follow the instructions as described in the earlier section "Formatting Cells."

CHAPTER 6

Working with E-Mail in Outlook

One of the most popular features of the **Internet** is electronic mail, or **e-mail** for short. **Microsoft Outlook 2000** is a powerful and easy-to-use component of Office 2000 that provides advanced e-mail and contact management features. Outlook also includes calendar, task management, and notes features that we'll investigate in Chapter 7. This chapter covers the following e-mail topics:

- How e-mail works
- Setting up Outlook for e-mail
- Using Outlook for e-mail
- Working with contacts
- Organizing in Outlook
- Working with newsgroups

---

 *Chapter 8 describes how to set up an Internet connection and how to use another popular area of the Internet, the **World Wide Web**, to share information.*

 Chapter 7 describes how to use Outlook to manage your personal information, including your calendar and to-do list.

How E-Mail Works

E-mail works like this: You use a **program** such as Outlook to create your message. Then you tell your e-mail program to send the message to your e-mail post office (which, technically, is called a mail server). Your e-mail post office then sends the message to the recipient's e-mail post office (technically, another mail server). The next time the recipient's e-mail **client** "visits" the e-mail post office to check for new mail, the recipient receives the e-mail message.

 E-mail programs are often called e-mail clients.

Before you can send someone an e-mail message, you need to know the person's e-mail name and address. This e-mail name and address identifies both the person you're sending the message to and the mail server that the person uses to pick up his or her e-mail messages. The following example shows how simple this process is.

 To be picky, you don't actually have to know the name of the recipient's mail server; you need to know only the name of the domain of the network of computers the person uses to connect to the Internet.

Suppose you want to send a message to the president of the United States. To do this, you need to know the domain name that the White House uses for its e-mail and you need to know the e-mail name that the White House uses to identify the president's e-mail mailbox. It turns out that the president's full e-mail name and address is *president@whitehouse.gov.* So the president's e-mail name is *president,* and the White House domain name is *whitehouse.gov.* The e-mail name and the domain name are separated by the @ symbol.

 When someone verbally gives an e-mail name and address, they say "at" in place of the @ symbol and "dot" in place of the period. So to describe the president's e-mail name and address, say "president at whitehouse dot gov." Note, however, that the actual e-mail name and address you type is president@whitehouse.gov.

That's really all you need to know to understand and use e-mail. To review, you use e-mail to send and receive electronic messages. To send someone an e-mail message, you need to know the person's e-mail name and address. Figure 6-1 shows a sample e-mail message created using Outlook.

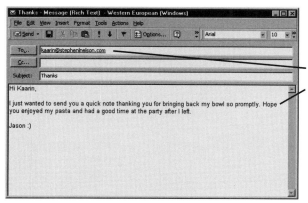

FIGURE 6-1

Most e-mail messages are short text messages.

This is the e-mail address.

This is the message text.

Setting Up Outlook for E–Mail

Before you use Outlook, you need to run the Outlook Startup **Wizard**, which helps you set up Outlook for the e-mail services you use. To use the Outlook Startup Wizard, follow these steps:

Notes *You also need to have an Internet connection set up on your PC. Chapter 8 describes how to do this.*

1 Start Outlook by **double-clicking** the Outlook icon on the desktop, or by **clicking** the Start button, pointing to Programs, and then clicking Microsoft Outlook.

*If you have never set up your Inbox, the Inbox Setup Wizard starts. Select Internet E-Mail and any other services you want, and then click Next. Click Setup Mail Account, and then enter your mail account information in the General, Servers, and Connections tabs of the **dialog box.** If you don't know what to enter in one of the wizard's dialog boxes, contact your Internet service provider. Click OK, enter the location where you would like to store your mail **files,** and click Next.*

2 If you have a previous version of Outlook and you want to keep its settings, click Yes and then click Next to finish the setup process. Otherwise click No, and then click Next.

3 If you currently use a different e-mail program and you want to import your messages, address book, and settings, select the program from the list of installed e-mail programs, as shown in Figure 6-2, and then click Next to finish. Otherwise, click None Of The Above, and click Next.

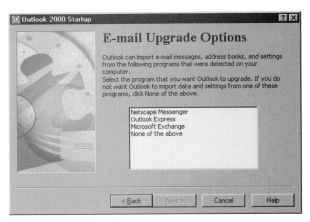

FIGURE 6-2

Choose the e-mail program you previously used to import your data into Outlook.

4 Click the Internet Only option button if you don't need access to a **Microsoft Exchange Server**, or click the Corporate Or Workgroup option button if you do (see Figure 6-3).

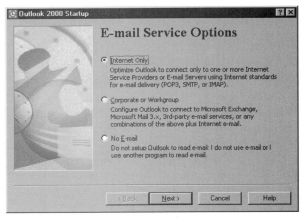

FIGURE 6-3

The e-mail service options for Outlook.

5 Click Next to finish setting up Outlook. If Outlook asks you for the location of your Personal Folders file, select the default directory, or select a **subfolder** in the My Documents **folder** to make backing up your files easier.

Using Outlook for E-Mail

After you set up Outlook, you're ready to begin using e-mail. This section describes how to use Outlook to accomplish the most important e-mailing tasks: reading e-mail messages, creating and delivering e-mail messages, building a list of e-mail contacts, replying to and forwarding e-mail messages, deleting e-mail messages, and e-mailing files in messages.

Reading E-Mail Messages

To read your e-mail messages in Outlook, click the Inbox folder. Outlook lists your messages in the Folder Contents pane and shows a message in the Preview pane, as shown in Figure 6-4.

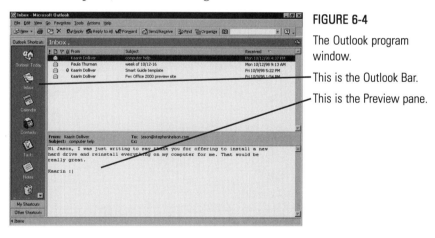

FIGURE 6-4

The Outlook program window.

This is the Outlook Bar.

This is the Preview pane.

 *To turn the Preview pane on or off, choose the View **menu's** Preview Pane command.*

To display the first three lines of unread messages in the Folder Contents pane, choose the View menu's AutoPreview command.

 Adding names to your Contacts folder for the people you frequently correspond with makes it quicker to e-mail them, as described in the later section "Working with Contacts."

If you want to open a new window especially for a message—perhaps so you can see more of the message—double-click the message in the Folder Contents pane. Outlook opens a window for the message. After you read the message, click the Close button.

Creating E-Mail Messages

To create an e-mail message using Outlook, follow these steps:

1 Start Outlook by double-clicking the Outlook icon on the desktop to display a window similar to that shown previously in Figure 6-4.

2 Click the New Message **toolbar** button to display a new Message window, as shown in Figure 6-5.

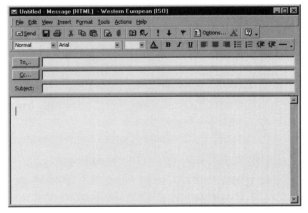

FIGURE 6-5

A blank Message window.

3 Enter the e-mail name and address of the message recipient in the To box. For example, if you're sending the president of the United States an e-mail message, type *president@whitehouse.gov* in the To box.

 If you already have an e-mail address in your Contacts folder for the person to whom you want to send an e-mail, click the To button to select the contact from a list.

4 Optionally, if you want to send a copy of the message to someone else, enter the e-mail address of the message copy recipient in the Cc box.

 You can send a message or message copy to more than one recipient by entering e-mail addresses separated by semicolons.

5 Type a brief description of the message subject in the Subject box.

6 Type your message. Figure 6-6 shows a message.

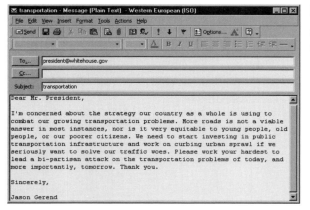

FIGURE 6-6

A message to the president of the United States.

6

7 Optionally, use the Message window's toolbar buttons to format your message. Note, however, that the recipient must use an e-mail client program (like Outlook) that understands how to display any formatting you apply. For this reason, it's often best not to format messages.

*To change the default message format, choose the Tools menu's Options command and then click the Mail Format tab. Select a mail format from the drop-down list box. Many modern e-mail programs support **HTML**-formatted e-mail, but not all. Plain Text is the safest format, although Rich Text usually works also.*

 To check the spelling in your message, choose the Tools menu's Spelling command. If Outlook finds an incorrectly spelled word, it displays a dialog box that lets you correct the misspelling.

8   When you finish typing your message, click the Send toolbar button to place the message in your Outbox folder.

 Placing a message in the Outbox folder doesn't actually send the message. You need to connect to the Internet and deliver the message to your mail server in order to actually send the message.

Delivering E-Mail Messages

To deliver the messages in your Outbox folder to your outgoing mail server, click the Send/Receive toolbar button or choose the Tools menu's Send/Receive command. If you aren't currently connected to the Internet, **Microsoft Windows** makes the connection. Then Windows delivers your outgoing messages and retrieves any incoming messages.

 If you have a direct connection to the Internet—perhaps through a local area network—Outlook automatically delivers a message when you click the Send toolbar button.

Replying to E-Mail Messages

You can send a reply message to someone who's sent you a message. To reply to a message, follow these steps:

1   Open the message.

2   Click the Reply toolbar button. When you do this, Outlook creates a new message for you, filling in the To box with the e-mail name and address of the person to whom you're replying, as shown in Figure 6-7. Outlook also fills in the Subject box for you and then copies the original message text.

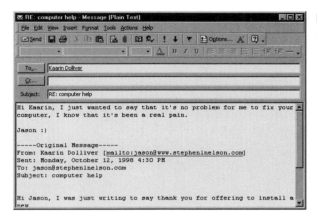

FIGURE 6-7

Replying to a message.

3 Add any new text to the message.

4 Delete any unneeded text from the original message text.

5 Click the Send toolbar button.

6 Deliver the message in the usual way.

  To reply to a message without including the original message text, choose the Tools menu's Options command, click E-Mail Options, and then select Do Not Include Original Message from the When Replying To A Message drop-down list box.

  To reply to a message and send a copy of your reply to every recipient of the original message, click the Reply To All toolbar button or choose the Actions menu's Reply To All command.

Forwarding E-Mail Messages

You can easily forward a copy of any message you receive to someone else. To forward a message, follow these steps:

1 Open the message.

2 Click the Forward Message toolbar button, or choose the Compose menu's Forward command. When you do this, Outlook creates a new message for you, filling in the Subject box and then copying the original message text, as shown in Figure 6-8.

3 Enter the e-mail name and address of the message recipient in the To box.

4 Add any new text to the message.

5   Click the Send toolbar button.

6   Connect to the Internet, and deliver the message in the usual way, if necessary.

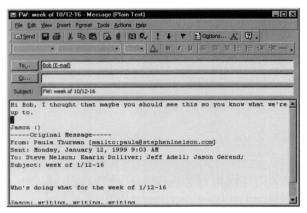

FIGURE 6-8

Forwarding a message.

 The people to whom you send messages can also easily forward them to anyone else. For this reason, you probably don't want to say anything in an e-mail message that you don't want repeated in public.

Deleting E-Mail Messages

To delete a message in one of the Outlook folders, select it and then click the Delete toolbar button or press the Delete key. You can also right-click the message and choose the shortcut menu's Delete command.

When you delete a message, Outlook moves the message to the Deleted Items folder. If you accidentally delete a message, you can still retrieve it. To retrieve a message, display the contents of the Deleted Items folder and then **drag** the message to a folder on the Outlook Bar or in the Folder List.

Because Outlook moves every message you delete to the Deleted Items folder, the number of messages stored in this folder grows quickly. To empty the Deleted Items folder, follow these steps:

1   Right-click the Deleted Items folder.

2   Choose the shortcut menu's Empty "Deleted Items" Folder command.

After you delete messages from the Deleted Items folder or empty the folder, the messages are permanently erased.

 To automatically empty the Deleted Items folder every time you close Outlook, choose the Tools menu's Options command, click the Other tab, and then select the Empty The Deleted Items Folder Upon Exiting check box.

E-Mailing a File Attachment

Although many e-mail messages include only text, it's also possible to e-mail files. When you e-mail a file, you simply attach a copy of the file to the message.

To e-mail a file **attachment**, follow these steps:

1 Click the New Message toolbar button to display the New Message window.

2 Enter the e-mail name and address of the message recipient in the To box.

3 To send a copy of the message to someone else, enter the e-mail name and address of a message copy recipient in the Cc box.

4 Type a brief description of the message subject in the Subject box.

5 Type your message.

6 Click the Insert File toolbar button, or choose the Insert menu's File command to display the Insert File dialog box, as shown in Figure 6-9.

FIGURE 6-9

The Insert File dialog box.

To insert the contents of a text file into your e-mail as text, in the Insert File dialog box click the down arrow next to the Insert button and then choose Insert As Text. Note that you would probably do this only with a short text file.

7   Select the disk that contains the file you want from the Look In drop-down list box, and locate the folder that contains the file you want to attach in the large list box.

8   Double-click the file you want to attach to the message. Outlook attaches the file to the message, as shown in Figure 6-10.

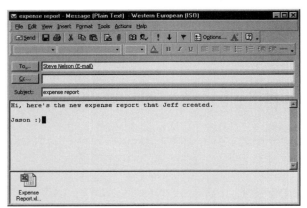

FIGURE 6-10

The Message window with message text and a file attachment.

 To e-mail files, both the e-mail client programs and the mail servers need to know how to handle the file attachments.

 If the message recipient uses different software than you do, you might need to convert the file to the correct format before you send it. The "Importing and Exporting" section in Chapter 1 describes how to save files in different formats.

If you receive a message with a file attachment, you can detach the file attachment from the message and permanently save the attachment. To do this, follow these steps:

1   Double-click the message header in the Folder Contents pane to display the message in its own window.

2   Right-click the attachment icon.

3 Choose the shortcut menu's Save As command to display the Save As dialog box.

4 Name the file, and specify in which folder it should be saved in the Save As dialog box.

 Notes *Chapter 1 describes how to save files.*

 Notes *If you want to only open a file attachment—not save it—you can do so by double-clicking its icon.*

Creating Signatures

People often create a block of standardized text called a signature which they can easily append to the end of e-mail messages rather than typing the information in every message. For example, a signature often includes the person's name, e-mail address, phone number, and maybe even a favorite saying. To create and add a signature to an e-mail message, follow these steps:

1 Choose the Tools menu's Options command.

2 Click the Mail Format tab.

3 Click Signature Picker.

4 Click New.

5 Type a name for your signature in the text box, and then click Next.

6 Type your text, and then click Finish (see Figure 6-11).

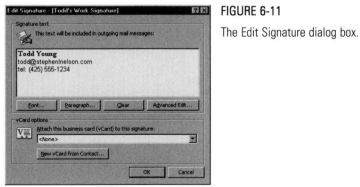

FIGURE 6-11

The Edit Signature dialog box.

*To attach your contact information as a part of your signature, click New vCard From Contact, select your own contact entry, and then click OK. Note that the recipient will need to use an e-mail program that supports the vCard standard, such as Outlook, **Microsoft Outlook Express**, or Netscape Messenger.*

7 Click OK to choose the selected signature.

8 Click OK to automatically include your signature in all messages, or select None from the Use This Signature By Default drop-down list box to prevent this.

Attaching Signatures

To attach a signature you've created to an e-mail message, follow these steps:

1 Click the New Message toolbar button to create a new message.

2 Choose the Insert menu's Signature command, and then choose the signature you want to insert from the submenu, as shown in Figure 6-12.

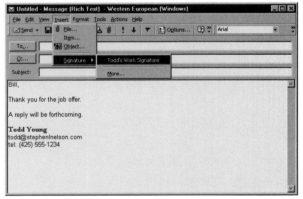

FIGURE 6-12

Attaching a signature to an e-mail.

Using Digital Signatures

E-mail has the potential to be a damaging medium of communication because unethical people can easily impersonate you and write things that you never said. **Digital signatures** can help prevent this situation by providing a secure "signature" which states that you wrote the e-mail.

To use a digital signature, you first need to acquire a **digital ID**, or certificate. A digital ID allows you to create a digital signature. To acquire a digital ID, choose the Tools menu's Options command, click the Security tab, and then click Get A Digital ID. This takes you to a web site where you can get a free trial digital ID or pay for a fully licensed ID.

After you download and install your digital ID, you need to enable your digital ID in Outlook. To do this, follow these steps:

1 Choose the Tools menu's Options command.

2 Click the Security tab, and then click Setup Secure E-Mail.

3 Type a name for your security settings in the Security Settings Name text box, as shown in Figure 6-13.

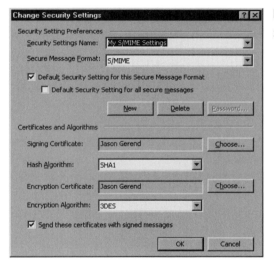

FIGURE 6-13

Setting up digital signatures.

4 Click OK.

5 Select the check boxes in the Secure E-Mail section of the tab to specify whether you want to encrypt messages, whether you want to attach your digital signature to all messages, and whether people should be allowed to read your messages even if their e-mail programs don't support digital signatures, as shown in Figure 6-14.

FIGURE 6-14

Specifying digital signature options.

6 Click OK.

If you uninstall Outlook, you lose your digital ID. To prevent this, or to copy your digital ID to another computer, choose the Tools menu's Options command, click the Security tab, and then click Import/Export Digital ID. Select the Export Your Digital ID To A File option, click Select to choose your digital ID, and then specify where to save the ID. Click OK when you're finished.

To attach a digital signature to your e-mail messages, follow these steps:

1 Click the New Message toolbar button to create a new message.

2 Click the Options toolbar button to display the Message Options dialog box.

3 Select the check boxes in the Security section to encrypt or digitally sign your message, as shown in Figure 6-15.

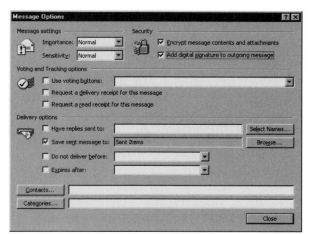

FIGURE 6-15

Attaching a digital signature and encrypting a message.

4 Click Close.

Not all e-mail programs support digital signatures and encryption. Microsoft Outlook and Outlook Express do, but Qualcomm's Eudora and Netscape's Messenger support different standards and so cannot accept messages signed or encrypted in Outlook.

Working with Contacts

As soon as you start working with e-mail in Outlook, you'll want to begin building a list of contacts in Outlook's Contacts folder. Using the Contacts folder to store names and e-mail addresses makes the task of addressing the e-mail messages you create quick and easy and reduces your chances of incorrectly addressing a message.

Adding People to Your Contacts Folder

To add a person's e-mail name and address to your Contacts folder if you've received a message from the person, follow these steps:

1 Double-click the message in the Folder Contents pane. Outlook opens a Message window for the message.

2 Right-click the From e-mail name and address information.

3 Choose the shortcut menu's Add To Contacts command, as shown in Figure 6-16.

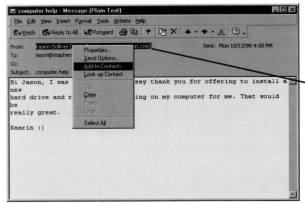

FIGURE 6-16

A Message window with the shortcut menu displayed.

Right-click here.

4 When Outlook displays the Contact dialog box, enter any additional information you know about the contact and then click the Save And Close toolbar button.

 If you add the name of a person who is already in your Contacts folder, when you save the contact, Outlook gives you the option to merge any new data with the old contact.

 *If you use Outlook to schedule meetings and the contact you're creating has **Free/Busy information** published on a web site, make sure you include the web site's **URL** in the contact information. To do this, click the Details tab and then type the URL of the Internet Free/Busy information in the Address text box at the bottom of the dialog box.*

 Chapter 7 describes how to schedule meetings using Outlook.

To add a person's e-mail name and address to your Contacts folder if you haven't received a message from the person, follow these steps:

1 Click the Contacts icon on the Outlook Bar to open the Contacts folder, as shown in Figure 6-17.

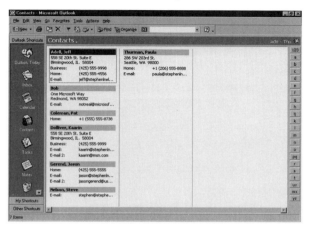

FIGURE 6-17

The Contacts folder shows the e-mail names and addresses you've collected.

2 Click the New Contact toolbar button to display a new Contact window, as shown in Figure 6-18.

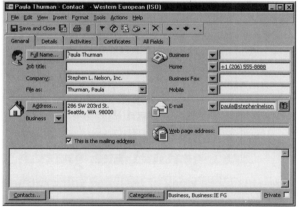

FIGURE 6-18

The Contact window.

3 Enter the person's name in the Full Name text box.

4 Enter the person's full e-mail name and address in the E-Mail text box.

5 Enter any additional information in the phone numbers, Address, and Web Page Address text boxes.

6 Click the Save And Close toolbar button. Outlook adds the person's information to your Contacts folder.

Sending Messages to a Contact

To use a name you've stored in the Contacts folder, follow these steps:

1 Click the New Message toolbar button to display a new Message window.

2 Click To to display the Select Names dialog box, as shown in Figure 6-19.

 As long as a recipient's name is in the Contacts folder, you can enter it in the To box by simply typing the first couple of letters of the name and pressing the Tab key. If Outlook recognizes the name, it enters the name for you.

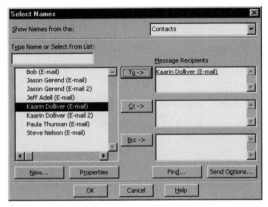

FIGURE 6-19

The Select Names dialog box shows the e-mail names you've collected.

3 To add a name to the To, Cc, or Bcc boxes, click the name to select it and then click the appropriate button.

 You can use the Bcc (Blind Carbon Copy) field to send a copy of the message to other people without the primary recipient's knowledge. However, the primary recipient could find out the names of the message copy recipients by displaying the message header—something that some e-mail programs do by default.

4 Click OK when you've finished selecting names. Then create your message in the usual way.

You can also send a message to a contact, as well as perform many other actions related to the contact, by selecting or opening a contact in the Contacts folder and choosing the Actions menu's New Message To Contact command or some other command.

Mapping a Contact's Address

Outlook allows you to use Microsoft Expedia Maps to create a map of a contact's address. To do this, follow these steps:

1 Double-click the contact whose address you want to map.

2 Click the Display Map Of Address toolbar button to connect to the Internet and display a map of the contact's address.

3 Use the **hyperlinks** on the **web page** to zoom in or out, print the map, or enlarge the map, as shown in Figure 6-20.

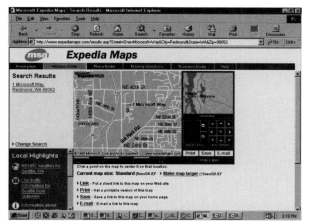

FIGURE 6-20

A contact's address mapped in Expedia Maps.

6

Changing the Look of the Contacts Folder

You can apply a number of different **views** to the Contacts folder to organize your contacts in a way that might be better suited to you. To change the view, choose the View menu's Current View command and then select a view from the submenu. Figure 6-21 shows the Contacts folder with the By Category view applied.

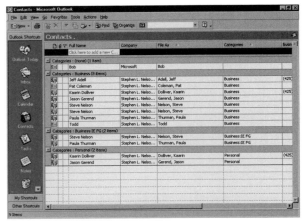

FIGURE 6-21

The Contacts folder viewed
by category.

 *You can further customize a view by choosing the View menu's Current
View command and the submenu's Customize Current View command.*

Table 6-1 describes the different views available. Experiment and see
which views you prefer.

View	What It Displays
Address Cards	The default, Rolodex-style address cards showing a summary of the contacts' information.
Detailed Address Cards	Rolodex-style address cards showing the contacts' information in detail.
Phone List	Contacts' names and phone numbers displayed in a list view.
By Category	Contacts grouped by category in a list view.
By Company	Contacts grouped by company in a list view.
By Location	Contacts grouped by location in a list view.
By Follow Up Flag	Contacts grouped by the type of follow-up flag attached to the contact in a list view.

TABLE 6-1: The views available for the Contacts folder.

Viewing Activities with a Contact

Sometimes it can be useful to have all the information you have regarding a contact in one spot: e-mails, appointments, tasks, notes, and so forth. Outlook provides the Activities tab in a Contact window just for this purpose. To view your activities with a contact, follow these steps:

1 Double-click the contact for which you want to view activities.

2 Click the Activities tab (see Figure 6-22).

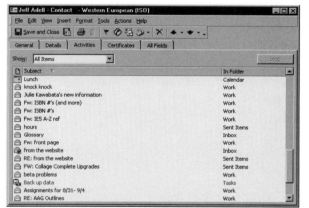

FIGURE 6-22

The Activities tab of a contact.

3 Select the type of items you want to view from the Show drop-down list box.

4 Double-click an item to open it.

Organizing in Outlook

If you're like most people, it's only a matter of time before your Inbox is bulging with messages, making it a chore to find the ones you want. Fortunately, Outlook allows you to move messages to other folders as well as to color-code messages from certain people and perform other organizational tasks.

Creating New Folders

To create a new folder for messages or other Outlook items, follow these steps:

1 Choose the File menu's New command and the submenu's Folder command.

2 Type a name for the folder in the Name text box, as shown in Figure 6-23.

FIGURE 6-23

The Create New Folder dialog box.

3 Select mail items from the Folder Contains drop-down list box to store e-mail messages, or select another option to store a different type of item.

4 Select the folder in which you want your new folder to be placed.

5 Click OK.

6 When Outlook asks if you want a shortcut to your folder added to the Outlook Bar, click Yes to create a new icon for your folder. Otherwise, click No.

Moving Messages to a Different Folder

To move a message to a new folder you've created, select the message and then drag it to the icon for the folder on the Outlook Bar.

If you don't have an icon for your folder on the Outlook Bar, follow these steps:

1 Click the Inbox icon on the Outlook Bar to open your Inbox.

2 Click the name of the currently open folder to display the Folder List, and then click the push-pin icon to keep the list open (see Figure 6-24).

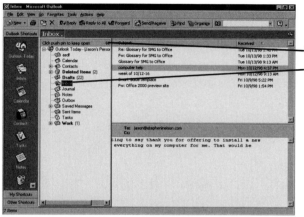

FIGURE 6-24

Displaying the Folder List.

The Push-pin icon.

Click here to display the Folder List.

3 Drag a message to the folder in the Folder List to which you want to move it.

 To close the Folder List, click the Close button in its pane.

 You can move and organize other types of items in the same way that you move and organize messages.

Automatically Moving Messages

To create a rule so that messages received from a particular person are automatically moved to a folder, follow these steps:

1 Click the Organize toolbar button.

2 Select a message from the person for whom you want to create a rule.

3 In the Organize pane, select the folder that you want to contain the person's messages, as shown in Figure 6-25.

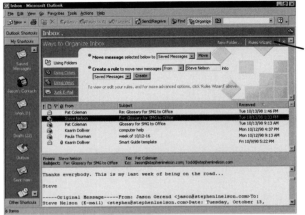

FIGURE 6-25

The Organize pane.

The Rules Wizard link.

4 Click Create.

 Click the Rules Wizard link at the top of the Organize pane to create and edit advanced rules in Outlook.

Automatically Coloring Messages

To create a rule so that messages you receive from a particular person are colored, follow these steps:

1 Click the Organize toolbar button.

2 Click the Using Colors tab in the Organize pane, as shown in Figure 6-26.

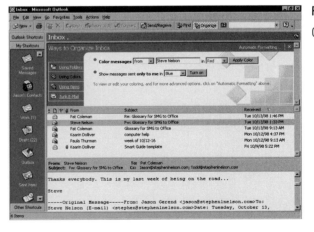

FIGURE 6-26

Coloring messages.

3 Select a message from the person for which you want to create a rule.

4 Select the color you want Outlook to automatically apply to messages from the selected person.

5 Click Apply Color.

Working with Newsgroups

Newsgroups are another way to share information over the Internet. In essence, a newsgroup works like a bulletin board in that people post messages for other people to read. Typically, you use a newsreader program to post and read the e-mail messages posted to a newsgroup. This section describes how to use Outlook Express, the newsreader program that comes with Office 2000 and **Microsoft Internet Explorer 5**.

Because there are perhaps hundreds of thousands of people who post messages on thousands of different topics and millions of people who want to read these messages, each newsgroup contains only those messages that fall into a specific category. For example, there's a newsgroup for fans of the Spice Girls, a newsgroup for people who enjoy fly-fishing, and a newsgroup devoted to topics on orchid cultivation. And as you might expect, there are hundreds and hundreds of newsgroups for specialty computer topics.

 Although Outlook Express is very similar to Outlook and has similar e-mail capabilities, you cannot directly access files stored in Outlook's folders from Outlook Express and vice versa. It's usually a good idea to use one program or the other for checking your e-mail and creating new messages, so you don't have messages scattered across two programs.

Subscribing to a Newsgroup

When you subscribe to a newsgroup, you can then easily visit the newsgroup and read or post messages. To subscribe to a newsgroup—which doesn't cost you anything, by the way—follow these steps:

1 Start Outlook Express by clicking the Start button, pointing to Programs and Internet Explorer, and then clicking Outlook Express.

2 Connect to the Internet if you aren't currently connected.

3 Select your news server in the Folder pane.

4 Click the Newsgroups toolbar button. Outlook Express lists all the newsgroups that your Internet service provider carries on that news server (see Figure 6-27).

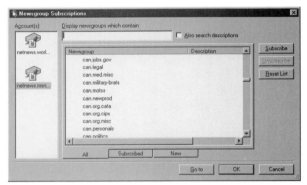

FIGURE 6-27

Outlook Express lists the newsgroups available on the news server.

5 Scroll through the list of newsgroups. When you find one to which you want to subscribe, double-click it. Then click Go To. You can subscribe to as many newsgroups as you want.

 To find newsgroups that cover a topic you're interested in, enter a topic name in the Display Newsgroups Which Contain text box. A list of newsgroups with the topic name appears.

Notes *Unfortunately, you can't tell from a newsgroup name what the newsgroup's messages are about. You'll need to experiment a bit—but that's part of the fun.*

Reading Newsgroup Messages

After you've subscribed to a newsgroup, you can then read the messages people have posted. To read a newsgroup's messages, follow these steps:

1 Click the newsgroup name in the Folder pane. If the news server branch of the list isn't expanded, you might need to do this by clicking the plus sign (+) to the left of the news server name. Outlook Express then retrieves a list of the newsgroup messages from the news server.

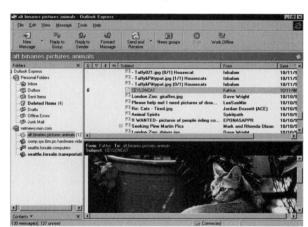

FIGURE 6-28

To read a newsgroup message, click or double-click the message.

2 Click the message you want to read in the Folder Contents pane. Outlook displays the message in the Preview pane. If you want to open a window for a message, double-click the message.

 Some newsgroup messages include file attachments. To save the file attachment that's part of a newsgroup message, right-click the attachment and then choose the shortcut menu's Save As command.

Posting a Newsgroup Message

To post a message to a newsgroup, first click the newsgroup name in the Folders List. Next click the New Message toolbar button. When Outlook displays a new Message window, enter a subject description in the box provided and then enter your message. (The steps for creating a newsgroup message closely resemble the steps for creating a regular e-mail message.) When you're finished, click the Send toolbar button to post your message to the newsgroup.

 If you post messages to newsgroups, you tend to receive lots of unsolicited e-mail from people who want to sell you various products and services—including many products or services that you might find offensive.

CHAPTER 7

Using Outlook for Your Calendar and Tasks

Microsoft Outlook 2000 is an extremely powerful tool for handling your day-to-day schedule and to-do list. Although I could write several chapters on Outlook's scheduling and task-management features alone, this chapter introduces the essential information you need to know to manage your life with Outlook by covering the following subjects:

- Using the Calendar
- Working with tasks
- Using notes

 Click *the Outlook Today icon on the Outlook Bar to see a summary of your schedule, tasks, and e-mail messages for the day.*

 *Chapter 6 has valuable information on how to use Outlook for **e-mail**, as well as how to keep names and contact information with the **Contacts** folder.*

 *Outlook also has a Journal feature you can use to record your activities, such as editing Office **documents**, making phone calls, and carrying on conversations. This book does not cover working with the Journal because, although it can be a useful tool for people who need to keep close track of many activities in their lives, for most people, the Activities tab in the Contacts **folder** is sufficient.*

Using the Calendar

You can use the Calendar folder in Outlook to schedule your time. Outlook breaks down the events of your day into three categories: Appointments, which can be any type of activity; Meetings, which involve getting together with others; and All Day Events, which are simply activities that take the whole day, but do not necessarily take time, such as a birthday.

Keeping your calendar in Outlook gives you the power to quickly view your schedule in varying detail, as well as the ability to correspond easily with others to plan meetings and appointments.

Viewing Your Calendar

You can view your Calendar in Outlook in any of a number of ways. To display the Calendar and change its **view**, follow these steps:

1 Click the Calendar icon on the Outlook Bar.

2 Select the number of days you want to view by clicking either the Day, Work Week, Week, or Month **toolbar** buttons, as shown in Figure 7-1.

 You can view any number of days you want by clicking the first day in the Date Navigator, holding down the Shift key, and then clicking the last day. To view nonadjacent days, hold down the Ctrl key while clicking dates in the Date Navigator.

 *You can choose other views from the View **menu's** Current View submenu or even customize a view by choosing the Current View submenu's Customize View command.*

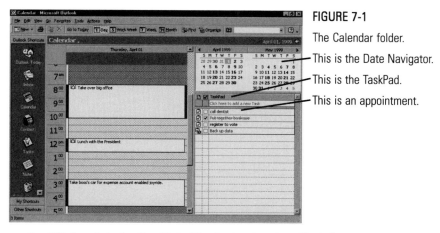

FIGURE 7-1

The Calendar folder.

This is the Date Navigator.

This is the TaskPad.

This is an appointment.

3 Click a date in the Date Navigator to view that day.

4 Click the Go To Today toolbar button to return to today's date.

*To quickly move to a distant month, click the month's name in the Date Navigator and **drag** the mouse up or down to the month you want to view.*

Notes

Using the TaskPad is an easy way to work with your tasks while viewing your Calendar. How to work with tasks is described in the later section "Working with Tasks."

Creating an Appointment

An important part of using Outlook to manage your schedule is making appointments. Appointments don't have to be with doctors and dentists; they can be any activity for which you want to schedule time: picking up groceries, writing a memo, commuting, and so on. To create an appointment, follow these steps:

1 Go to the date for which you want to schedule an appointment.

2 Click a free time during the day, and type a brief description of the appointment, as shown in Figure 7-2.

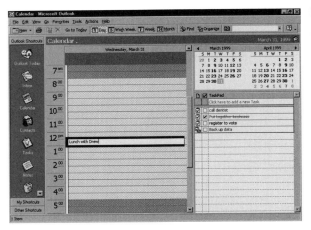

FIGURE 7-2

Creating an appointment.

3 To make the appointment longer, click the appointment and drag the bottom blue line down.

4 To move the appointment to a different time, click the appointment and drag it to the new time.

Editing an Appointment

After you've created an appointment, you might want to specify a location, set a reminder, or change how the time appears to others who might be viewing your schedule remotely. To edit an appointment's properties, follow these steps:

1 **Double-click** the appointment you want to edit.

2 Type where the appointment will take place in the Location text box, as shown in Figure 7-3.

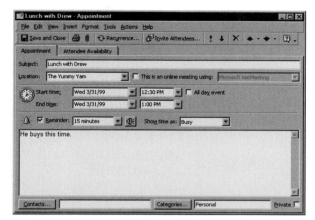

FIGURE 7-3

Editing an appointment.

3 Change the start and end times, if necessary, by typing a day or time in the Start Time and End Time boxes, or clicking the down arrows and selecting options from the drop-down lists.

4 Select the Reminder check box, and specify how much in advance of the appointment you want to be reminded.

5 If you make your schedule available to others across a network or on the **Internet,** indicate how you want the appointment to appear by selecting an option from the Show Time As drop-down list box.

6 Type any notes in the large text box.

7 Click Contacts or Categories to associate the appointment with a person or category.

8 Click the Save And Close toolbar button when you're finished.

Making an Appointment Recur

After you've created an appointment, you might want to make it a recurring appointment if it happens regularly at a set time and on a particular day. To make an appointment recur, follow these steps:

1   Double-click the appointment you want to recur.

2   Click the Recurrence toolbar button.

3   Enter the start and end times in the Start Time and End Time text boxes, as shown in Figure 7-4.

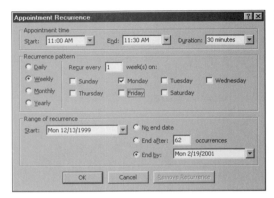

FIGURE 7-4

The Appointment Recurrence dialog box.

 You can type your own time, duration, or date in a box. You can also use words such as "now," to specify the current time, or "tomorrow," to use tomorrow's date.

4   Choose the recurrence pattern for the appointment by clicking either the Daily, Weekly, Monthly, or Yearly option button, and then selecting the days on which the appointment should recur.

5   Enter the starting date in the Start text box, or click the down arrow and select a date from the pop-up calendar.

6   Optionally, click the End After or End By options buttons and specify when the last appointment ends.

7   Click OK.

8   Click the Save And Close toolbar button.

Creating an All Day Event

Outlook calls any Appointment or Meeting that takes the whole day an All Day Event. All Day Events can be useful for recording such things as birthdays and anniversaries, which last all day but do not necessarily preclude you from making other appointments or meetings. To create an All Day Event, follow these steps:

1 Click the gray area above the day on which you want to schedule an All Day Event, as shown in Figure 7-5.

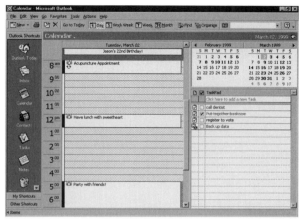

FIGURE 7-5

An All Day Event in the Calendar.

2 Type the subject for your event.

Creating a Meeting Request

You can request a meeting with someone by sending the person a meeting request. To create a meeting request, follow these steps:

1 Click the day and time on which you want to schedule the meeting.

2 Choose the Actions menu's New Meeting Request command.

3 Enter the e-mail name and address of the person with whom you want to meet in the To text box, or click To and select a name from your Contacts folder.

4 Fill in the appointment details as usual, making sure to type a message to the recipient in the large text box (see Figure 7-6).

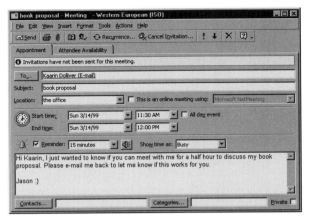

FIGURE 7-6

A Meeting Request window.

5 Click the Send toolbar button when you're finished.

The recipient of your meeting request will receive an e-mail listing the date and time of your requested meeting and the notes you typed in the large text box. If you don't include a message requesting your recipient's presence at your meeting, they won't know what to do.

To send your meeting request as an actual Calendar item that recipients can save to their own Calendars, create an appointment for your meeting, click the meeting, and then choose the Actions menu's Forward As ICalendar command. Create your e-mail message as usual, and click the Send toolbar button.

Planning a Meeting

If the people with whom you want to meet all have their **Free/Busy information** available on your local network with a **Microsoft Exchange Server**, or on a web site, you can use the Plan A Meeting tool to schedule a time that works for everyone. To do this, follow these steps:

1 Click the time in your Calendar when you would like to schedule a meeting.

2 Choose the Actions menu's Plan A Meeting command.

3 Click Invite Others.

4 Select the people who are required for the meeting, and click Required, as shown in Figure 7-7.

*You can only obtain schedule information for the people whose names you select from your Global Address List, if you're on an Exchange Server network, or for the people for whom you've recorded an **URL** for their Internet Free/Busy information.*

 To record a contact's Internet Free/Busy information, click the Contacts icon on the Outlook bar, double-click the contact, click the Details tab, and then type the Internet Free/Busy information URL in the Address text box.

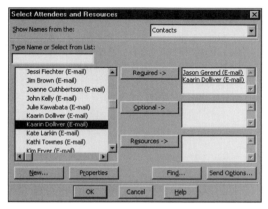

FIGURE 7-7

The Select Attendees And Resources dialog box.

5 Select any optional people and any resources necessary for the meeting (such as a conference room).

6 Click OK.

7 Click AutoPick, and specify who and what needs to be available for a meeting, as shown in Figure 7-8.

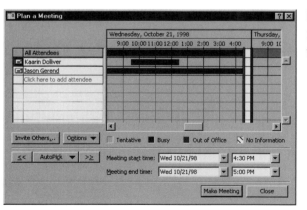

FIGURE 7-8

Use the Plan A Meeting tool to schedule meetings.

8 Click the forward arrows to search for a time that all attendees have free farther in the future, or click the backward arrows to search for a time closer to the present.

9 After finding a time that works, click Make Meeting.

10 Type the subject and location of the meeting, and then type a message in the large text box.

11 Click the Send toolbar button.

 The Plan A Meeting tool may not be very effective for planning meetings more than two months in advance because many people do not publish more than two months of their schedules.

Sending a Meeting Update

After you've scheduled a meeting and sent out invitations, you need to alert your attendees to any changes you make to a meeting. To send a meeting update, follow these steps:

1 Double-click the meeting in your Calendar.

2 Make any changes you want, as shown in Figure 7-9.

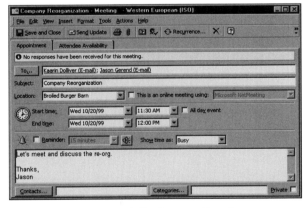

FIGURE 7-9

Sending a meeting update.

3 Click the Send Update toolbar button.

Canceling a Meeting

To cancel or delete a meeting, click the meeting in your Calendar and then click the Delete toolbar button. Click OK in the **dialog box** Outlook displays to notify attendees that the meeting has been canceled, or click the Delete Without Sending A Cancellation option button and then click OK to not tell any attendees about the cancellation (see Figure 7-10).

FIGURE 7-10

Canceling a meeting.

Printing Your Calendar

If you use a standard, paper-based day planner and you want to include your Outlook Calendar in it, or if you simply want a hard copy of your Calendar, Outlook can create printouts to meet your needs. To print your Calendar, follow these steps:

1 Choose the File menu's Print command.

2 Select a printer from the Name drop-down list box, as shown in Figure 7-11.

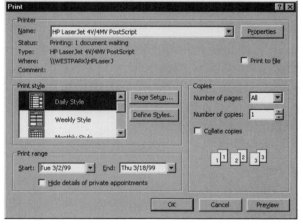

FIGURE 7-11

Printing the Calendar.

3 Select a style for your printout from the Print Style list box.

If you want to print dual-sided, select Odd from the Number Of Pages drop-down list box, and print your Calendar. Then take the pages and put them back in the printer tray upside down (consult your printer's documentation as to which way is upside down), select Even from the Number Of Pages drop-down list box, and print your Calendar again.

4 Specify starting and ending dates in the Start and End boxes.

5 Specify how many copies you want in the Number Of Copies box.

6 Click Preview to see a preview of your printout.

7 Click Print if you like the preview, or click Close to cancel.

Posting Your Free/Busy Information

Unless you're on a local network with an Exchange Server, you need to publish your Free/Busy information to a **web site** so people can use the Plan A Meeting tool or another calendar **program's** tools to view the times when you are free or busy. To publish your Internet Free/Busy information, follow these steps:

1 Choose the Tools menu's Options command.

2 Click Calendar Options.

3 Click Free/Busy Options to display the Free/Busy Options dialog box.

4 Select the Publish My Free/Busy Information check box, as shown in Figure 7-12.

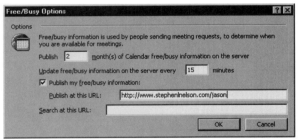

FIGURE 7-12

The Free/Busy Options dialog box.

5 Type the URL for your web site in the Publish At This URL text box.

6 Click OK.

Saving Your Calendar as a Web Page

Outlook can create elegant **web pages** from your Calendar information for posting on the Internet. To do this, follow these steps:

1 While viewing your Calendar, choose the File menu's Save As Web Page command.

2 Select the dates you want published from the Start Date and End Date boxes, as shown in Figure 7-13.

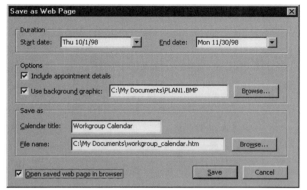

FIGURE 7-13

The Save As Web Page dialog box.

3 Select the Include Appointment Details check box to show the appointment subject and location.

4 Select the Use Background Graphic check box, and then click Browse to select a picture to use as the background for your web page.

5 Select the image you want to use, and then click Select.

6 Type a title for the web page in the Calendar Title text box.

7 Type a **filename** in the File Name text box, and then click Browse to select the folder in which you want to save it.

8 Select the folder, and click Select.

9 Click Save.

Working with Tasks

The Tasks folder in Outlook is where you can keep track of your to-do list. When you use Outlook to keep your tasks list, you can easily sort tasks, categorize tasks, assign tasks to other people, and send status reports on the progress you make on your own tasks.

 You can do everything in the Calendar folder's TaskPad that you can do in the Tasks folder itself.

Creating Tasks

To create a task in the Tasks folder or in the TaskPad, follow these steps:

1 Click where it says *Click Here To Add A New Task,* and type the subject for your new task, as shown in Figure 7-14.

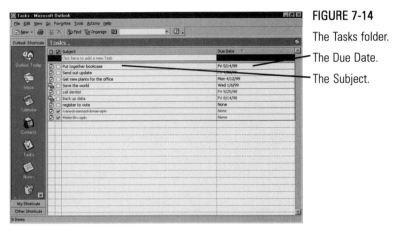

FIGURE 7-14

The Tasks folder.

The Due Date.

The Subject.

2 Type a due date in the Due Date text box if you have a deadline for your task.

3 Press the Enter key.

 You can also click the New Task toolbar button to create a new task.

Editing Tasks

To add or change information about a task you've created, follow these steps:

 If you need to change only the subject or due date, you can click the field you want to change in the tasks list and enter a new subject or date.

1 Double-click the task you want to edit.

2 Edit the subject by typing new text in the Subject text box, as shown in Figure 7-15.

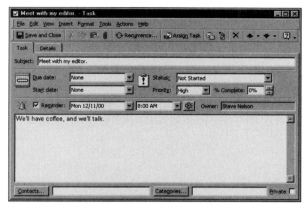

FIGURE 7-15

Editing a task using the Task window.

3 Enter dates in the Due Date and Start Date boxes for when the task should begin and when it is due.

4 Describe your progress in the Status and % Complete boxes.

5 Select the Reminder check box, and specify a day and time if you want to be reminded of the task.

6 Type any notes in the large text box.

7 Click Contacts or Categories to associate the task with certain people or categories.

8 Click the Save And Close toolbar button when you're finished.

Checking Tasks as Completed

After you've finished a task, you will probably want to mark it as completed. To do so, select the check box to the left of the task Subject in the Tasks list, as shown in Figure 7-16.

To delete a task, click the task and then click the Delete toolbar button.

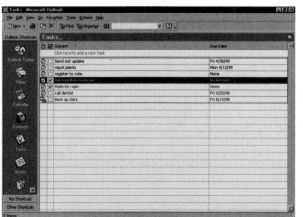

FIGURE 7-16

Checking off a task in the Tasks folder.

Outlook immediately deletes the task when you click the Delete toolbar button. If you change your mind and want to recover a deleted task, you need to open the Deleted Items folder.

Changing the Tasks View

You can easily change the way you view your tasks in Outlook to display the task information that is most important to you or to make it easier to categorize and sort your tasks. To do this, choose the View menu's Current View command, and then choose a view from the submenu. Figure 7-17 shows the By Category view.

 You can further customize your view by choosing the View menu's Current View command and the submenu's Customize Current View command .

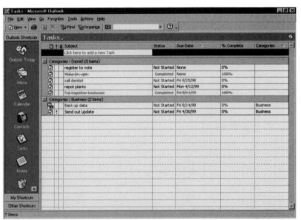

FIGURE 7-17

The Tasks folder with the By Category view applied.

Table 7-1 describes the different views available. Try them out and see which one suits you best.

View	What It Displays
Simple List	Task check-off, subject, and due-date fields.
Detailed List	Priority, **attachments,** subject, status, due-date, % complete and categories fields.
Active Tasks	All tasks that have passed their start dates displayed in Detailed List view.

View	What It Displays
Next Seven Days	All tasks that will be active during the next seven days displayed in Detailed List view.
Overdue Tasks	All overdue tasks displayed in Detailed List view.
By Category	Tasks grouped by category displayed in Detailed List view.
Assignment	All assignments you have displayed in Detailed List view.
By Person Responsible	All tasks grouped by owner with priority, attachments, subject, requested by, owner, due-date, and status fields displayed.
Completed Tasks	Completed tasks with priority, attachments, subject, due-date, date completed, and categories fields displayed.
Task Timeline	All tasks shown on a timeline with start dates and due dates displayed.

TABLE 7-1: The views available for the Tasks folder.

Assigning Tasks to Others

To assign a task you've created to someone else, follow these steps:

1 Double-click the task you want to assign.

2 Click the Assign Task toolbar button.

3 Enter the e-mail name and address of the person to whom you want to assign the task in the To text box, or click To to select a name from your Contacts folder (see Figure 7-18).

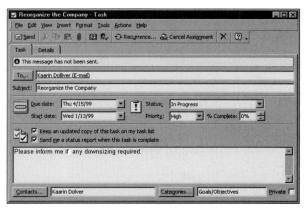

FIGURE 7-18

Assigning a task to another person.

4 Click the Send toolbar button.

Chapter 6 describes how to use Outlook for e-mail.

Sending Status Reports

To create and send an e-mail message that details your progress on a task, follow these steps:

1 Double-click the task you want to report on.

2 Choose the Actions menu's Send Status Report command.

3 Enter the e-mail names and addresses in the To and Cc fields for the recipients of your status report.

4 Type any additional text in the message body, as shown in Figure 7-19.

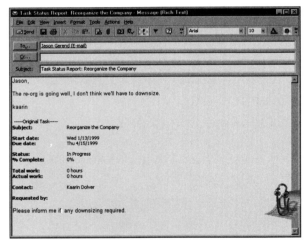

FIGURE 7-19

Sending a status report.

5 Click the Send toolbar button.

Using Notes

Notes are the computer equivalent to the sticky notes you put on your fridge or computer monitor; they're small and yellow and you can record short little notes on them. Outlook improves on the sticky note by allowing you to edit your notes, save them, e-mail them, and even change their color.

Creating Notes

To create a note, follow these steps:

1 Click the Notes icon on the Outlook Bar.

2 Click the New Note toolbar button.

3 Type your note, as shown in Figure 7-20.

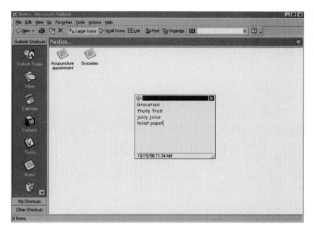

FIGURE 7-20

The Notes folder and a new note.

4 Leave the note open, or click the Close button to save it to the Notes folder.

 Notes are part of the Outlook program. When you leave notes open after closing Outlook, most of the Outlook program remains in system memory, taking up resources. If you have many programs open and do not have much RAM, you might want to close notes when you don't need them.

 To delete a note you no longer want, click the Delete toolbar button.

Printing Notes

To print a note, follow these steps:

1 Select a note from the Notes folder, and then choose the File menu's Print command.

2 Select your printer from the Name drop-down list box.

3 Specify the number of copies in the Number Of Copies box.

4 Click Preview to check that your note will print the way you want.

5 Click Print in the Preview window to print or click Close to cancel.

Changing Note Properties

To change the appearance of a note, or to associate the note with a contact or category, follow these steps:

1 Double-click a note in the Notes folder to open the note.

2 Choose the note's control menu's Color command, and then choose a color to recolor your note, as shown in Figure 7-21.

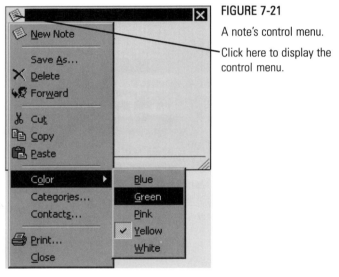

FIGURE 7-21

A note's control menu.

Click here to display the control menu.

3 Choose the control menu's Categories or Contacts command to assign a category or contact to the note.

Sending Notes

To send a note to someone, click the note in the Notes folder and then drag it to the Inbox icon on the Outlook Bar. This opens a new Message window with the contents of the note as the message. Compose and send your message as you would a normal e-mail message.

CHAPTER 8

Using Internet Explorer

Microsoft Office 2000 comes with **Microsoft Internet Explorer 5,** a powerful **web browser** that you can use to explore the **Internet**. In this chapter I introduce Internet Explorer and assist you in your explorations of the **World Wide Web** by discussing the following topics:

- Connecting to the Internet
- A World Wide Web primer
- Performing common tasks with Internet Explorer
- Working with **channels** and **offline pages**

Connecting to the Internet

Before you can begin using the Internet, you need to connect your computer to the Internet. Typically, the way that you do this is by using a telephone line and a modem. If this is the way you want to connect, you first need to describe how this connection will work and sign up for an account that lets you connect to the Internet.

 Using the Internet is free, but connecting to it usually isn't. Certain companies, called Internet service providers, or ISPs for short, let you access the Internet for a monthly fee. If you think of the Internet as an information superhighway, the ISPs charge entrance fees at the on-ramps. Once you get on, however, you can go anywhere you want—regardless of whether your destination is New York or Nigeria—for free. Only a few destinations charge visiting fees.

 If you work on a computer that has a permanent connection to the Internet, such as through a local area network, you don't need to dial up using a modem in order to use the Internet. You're already connected to the Internet. If you have questions about how this permanent connection works, ask your network administrator.

You can use the Internet **Connection Wizard** that comes with **Microsoft Windows** 98 and Internet Explorer to set up an Internet connection. To do so, follow these steps:

1 **Click** the Start button.

2 Point to Programs, Internet Explorer, and then click Connection Wizard to start the **wizard** you'll use to set up and describe your Internet connection, as shown in Figure 8-1.

 If you have a Connect To The Internet icon on your desktop, you can also double-click this icon to start the Connection Wizard.

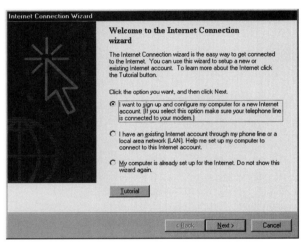

FIGURE 8-1

Use the Internet Connection Wizard command to set up and describe an Internet connection.

3 Click the option button that indicates you want to sign up and configure your computer for a new Internet account. Then click Next.

4 The Connection Wizard connects to the Internet to retrieve a list of ISPs that provide service to your area (see Figure 8-2).

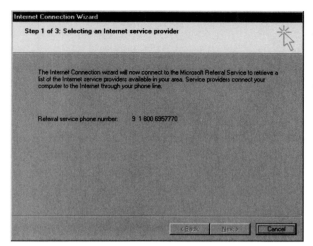

FIGURE 8-2

The Connection Wizard will retrieve a list of ISPs that provide service to your area.

5 When the Connection Wizard displays its list of ISPs, read through the descriptions, click to select the one you want, and then click Next.

The Internet service providers listed in the Connection Wizard most likely make up only a fraction of the ISPs available in your area. You don't have to choose one of the ISPs listed. Ask around for recommendations, and consider these factors before you choose an ISP. First, you want to make sure that whoever you choose provides good service. This means that the provider has enough phone lines so you can dependably make your connection. It also means that you can reach your ISP's technical support technicians when you need help. Second, you want to determine the costs of making your connection. This means confirming that the connection requires only a local telephone call (not a long distance call). Third, you need to consider cost. Most ISPs offer inexpensive plans, but these plans usually include only a few hours of connection time. Consider one of the unlimited usage plans if you anticipate that you, your co-workers, or your family members will spend a lot of time connected to the Internet. And last, if you think you might want to create your own presence on the World Wide Web (described later in this chapter), you need to make sure that your account includes space on the server to host a **web page**.

If you want to use an ISP not listed in the Connection Wizard, you can still use the Connection Wizard to set up your connection. Just click the second option button when you start the wizard, and then follow the steps to provide the information that your ISP gave you. If you have any questions, contact your ISP.

6   Follow the Connection Wizard's onscreen instructions. You'll be asked to provide your name, address, and credit card number, as well as some other information. After you complete these instructions—and different ISPs have you step through a slightly different process—you've set up the Dial-Up Networking connection you'll use to connect to the Internet.

 *Think carefully about the **e-mail** name you request. You want to pick a name that you can easily describe or provide. For example, something like "joe" is good because you'll later be able to say, "Oh, my e-mail name is 'joe'." Something cryptic like "jgl482" is not good because you'll often find it difficult to provide this name to people.*

You usually don't need to do anything special to initiate your new Internet connection. When you start Internet Explorer, the **program** prompts you to make a connection. For example, it might require you to log on by entering your account name and **password.** After you log on the first time, you can usually select a check box to have Windows enter your user name and password automatically so you don't have to do so in the future.

If you aren't automatically asked to connect and you want to make a manual connection, follow these steps:

1   Click the Start button.

2   Point to Programs, Accessories, and Communications.

3   Click Dial-Up Networking to display the Dial-Up Networking window, as shown in Figure 8-3.

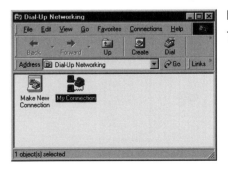

FIGURE 8-3

The Dial-Up Networking window.

4 Double-click the icon for the connection you want to make to display the connection's Connect To **dialog box**, as shown in Figure 8-4.

FIGURE 8-4

The Connect To dialog box for a generic ISP.

5 Confirm your user name and password, and click Connect.

A World Wide Web Primer

Let's open the discussion about the Internet with the most talked about part of it—the World Wide Web. The World Wide Web lets you view special **files**, called web pages, connected to each other with clickable **hyperlinks.** The Web is very easy to use—much easier than e-mail, for example. However, just to make sure you're comfortable with the concepts, let's go over a few points.

Understanding the Web

As noted above, the Web consists of web pages connected by hyperlinks. To understand this definition, you need to know the meaning of two key terms, *web page* and *hyperlink.*

A web page is a file that typically uses multiple media for communicating information. For example, text is one medium. Pictures are another. Sound is still another. So web pages are files that use text, pictures, and sometimes even sound. Figure 8-5 shows a National Hockey League web page. Note that it uses multiple media—both text and pictures. Web pages are the building blocks of the Web. A group of web pages linked together and stored in the same place make up a **web site.** For example, the National Hockey League web site is made up of several web pages. Some pages list teams and players, some list schedules, and others contain video clips or let you purchase products.

The unique feature of web pages is that they also include hyperlinks. A hyperlink, essentially, is an address that points to another Internet resource such as a web page. When you click a hyperlink, you're actually telling Windows to retrieve and then display the resource identified by the hyperlink. In Figure 8-5, for example, there are several hyperlinks. The words across the top of the web page are hyperlinks. All of the underlined segments of text are hyperlinks as well.

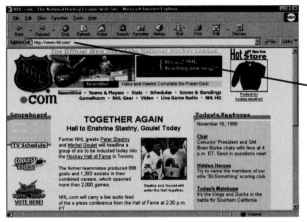

FIGURE 8-5

The main web page of the National Hockey League web site.

The web page address appears in the Address box.

If you click the Teams & Players hyperlink, your web browser retrieves a web page with links to pages for every team in the league, as shown in Figure 8-6.

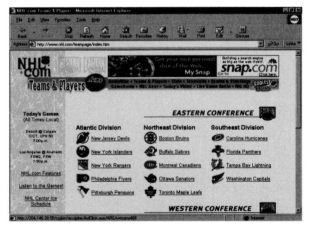

FIGURE 8-6

This web page appears when you click the Teams & Players hyperlink.

You now know how to view web pages and work with hyperlinks. But you should also learn how addresses work so you can use them as you browse web pages.

A web page address is made up of four parts:

- A code that identifies the address as a World Wide Web page
- The name of the computer, called a web server, that stores the web page
- The folder location of the web page
- The web page name

If you look at Figure 8-6, you'll notice that its address is

http://www.nhl.com/teampage/index.htm

The *http://* part of this address is the code that identifies the address as a World Wide Web page. The *www.nhl.com* part of the address is the name of the National Hockey League web server. (Remember that this is just the computer that stores the web page.) The */teampage/* part of the address is the folder holding the web page. Finally, *index.htm* is the actual web page name.

 Web page addresses are also known by the term uniform resource locator, *or* **URL**.

Basic Web Navigation Techniques

To view a web page, start Internet Explorer by clicking the Internet Explorer button on the Quick Launch toolbar located in the lower left corner of the desktop.

 The Quick Launch toolbar is only available if you are using Internet Explorer's web update feature.

If you aren't connected to the Internet, Windows might prompt you for the information it needs to make this connection. You might, for example, need to supply a password.

In any event, your web browser soon begins loading a home page such as the one shown in Figure 8-7, which is simply a default web page.

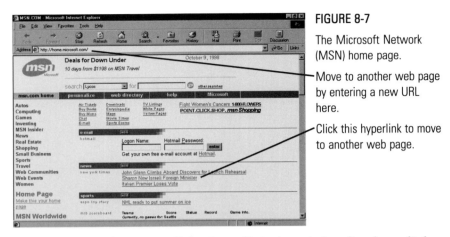

FIGURE 8-7

The Microsoft Network
(MSN) home page.

Move to another web page
by entering a new URL
here.

Click this hyperlink to move
to another web page.

To move to another page, click a hyperlink. As noted earlier, hyperlinks often appear as underlined text. They also appear as clickable buttons. You can always tell whether some bit of text is a hyperlink, however, by pointing to it. If you point to a hyperlink with the mouse, Windows changes the mouse pointer to a pointing finger.

You can also move to another web page by typing the web page's address, or URL, in the Address box. Note that you can return to your home page at any time by clicking the Home toolbar button.

When entering URLs, you don't need to enter the entire address. Web page addresses almost always begin with http://, so you can leave this part out. You can also leave out the last / of the address, if the address ends with one.

If you don't know the address for a site you want to visit on the World Wide Web, you can often successfully guess it. Here's how:

- Many URLs begin with the letters *www*. Enter this first, followed by a period.

- Enter the name of the business, organization, or institution next, followed by a period. Don't include spaces. If the name is very long, it's probably abbreviated. Think of any likely abbreviations.

- For U.S. web pages, enter the domain .com for a commercial organization, .gov for a governmental organization, .edu for an educational institution, .org for a nonprofit organization, or .mil for a military organization. Or if the page you want to display is international, enter the country's two-letter domain code.

This might take a few tries, but with a little trial and error, it often works.

Let me give you a couple of examples. Let's say you want to see the home page for the National Science Foundation. Here are a few URLs you might want to try:

www.science.gov

www.sciencefoundation.gov

www.nsf.gov

If one doesn't work, Internet Explorer either displays an incorrect page or beeps at you. You can then try the next URL. In this case, the third time's a charm.

Here's another example. Let's say you want to visit the home page for the Van Gogh Museum in Amsterdam. Here's what you might try:

www.vangoghmuseum.nl

And you'd be right!

You can also move between web pages in Internet Explorer by clicking two buttons labeled Back and Forward (see Figure 8-8). You can move to a web page you've previously viewed by clicking the Back toolbar button. After you click the Back toolbar button, you can move to the page you viewed before clicking Back by clicking the Forward toolbar button.

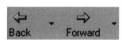

FIGURE 8-8

The Back and Forward buttons.

To tell Internet Explorer to stop loading a web page, click the Stop toolbar button (see Figure 8-9). You might want to stop loading a web page if retrieving the page is taking a long time—too long for you to wait.

To grab an updated copy of a web page, click the Refresh toolbar button (see Figure 8-9). You might want to do this if you're viewing a web page with information that changes frequently, or if you had to click Stop because the web page was taking too long to appear.

FIGURE 8-9

The Stop and Refresh buttons.

Performing Common Tasks with Internet Explorer

This next section describes how to work with some of the special features of Internet Explorer. You can also accomplish many of the tasks described here using a different web browser. Other web browsers work in similar ways.

Designating a Home Page

If you don't like the web page that appears each time you start Internet Explorer, you can tell Internet Explorer to display a different page (called a start page or a home page) at startup.

 Notes — *The term* home page *has three separate meanings. First, home page can describe the web page that initially appears when you start Internet Explorer. Second, you can create your own web page and call it your home page. And third, people and businesses who create multipage web sites use the term home page to describe the main web page of their web sites. This section of the chapter refers to the first definition of a home page.*

To change your home page, follow these steps:

1 Choose the Tools **menu's** Internet Options command to display the Internet Options dialog box, as shown in Figure 8-10.

2 In the Home Page section, enter the address of the web page you want to use as your home page in the Address box.

3 Click OK.

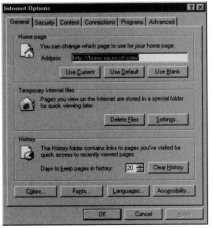

FIGURE 8-10

The Internet Options dialog box.

To display your home page, click the Home toolbar button. It's usually best to pick a web page for your home page that you most frequently visit or that you can easily use as a springboard to browse the World Wide Web. Many web sites allow you to customize your home page by choosing which information and hyperlinks you want included on the page.

Searching the Internet

Once you've spent a bit of time working with the Internet, you'll discover that with millions of resources available, you can't always easily find what you want. To address this problem, you'll want to learn how to use a search engine. Click Search to open the Search bar in Internet Explorer, as shown in Figure 8-11. The Search bar lets you perform a search while continuing to browse in the main frame of the Internet Explorer window.

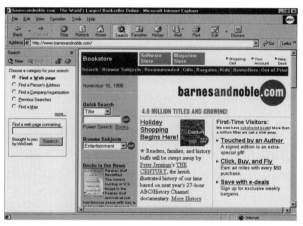

FIGURE 8-11

The Internet Explorer window with the Search bar displayed.

There are two types of search engines: directory-style search engines and index-style search engines. Directory-style search engines work like the Yellow Pages. You search through alphabetical lists organized by category. One of the most popular directory-style search engines is Yahoo!, which you can visit by entering its web page address, http://www.yahoo.com, in the Address box. Yahoo! has nowhere near an all-inclusive list of web sites, but instead it filters web sites and focuses on the largest and most popular.

Experiment on your own using Yahoo!'s categories to find a web page that provides content related to a hobby of yours or perhaps a school project of your kids'.

Index-style search engines build **databases** of keywords included in web pages, rather than sorting and filtering web pages by topic. One popular index-style search engine is HotBot, which you can visit by entering its web page address, http://www.hotbot.com, in the Address box, as shown in Figure 8-12.

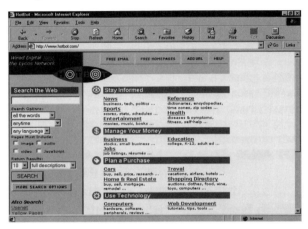

FIGURE 8-12

HotBot provides a web form you use to supply the word or phrase you want to look up.

To use an index-style search engine, type a word or phrase, click Search, and then wait for the search engine to build a list of web pages that use the word or phrase you typed. Figure 8-13 shows the first portion of a list of web pages that use the phrase "color blindness." To visit a web page, just click its hyperlink.

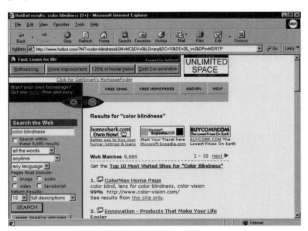

FIGURE 8-13

An index-style search engine builds a list of web pages that use the word or phrase you supplied.

Let me make a couple of final comments about search engines. First, a powerful search engine actually indexes millions and millions of web pages. Therefore, you commonly get a list of hundreds of web pages that use the word or phrase you supplied. Typically, an index-style search engine prioritizes the web pages it finds. It might, for example, list 25 web pages with the closest match on the first page of search results, 25 more web pages on the second page, and so on. In all cases, you usually need to do a bit of digging to find what you're looking for.

 At the bottom of each page of search results are hyperlinks that let you move to another page.

Second, numerous search engines exist. I've mentioned two already in this chapter, but there are many others. Table 8-1 lists some of the most popular search engines. You might want to visit and experiment with more than one of them.

Search Engine	Web Page Address
AltaVista	http://www.altavista.digital.com
Excite	http://www.excite.com
HotBot	http://www.hotbot.com
InfoSeek	http://www.infoseek.com
Lycos	http://www.lycos.com
MetaCrawler	http://www.metacrawler.com
WebCrawler	http://www.webcrawler.com
Yahoo!	http://www.yahoo.com

TABLE 8-1: Web page addresses of popular search engines.

8

 As you might expect, different search engines work differently. You'll find it well worth your effort to learn as much as you can about how to work with a specific search engine. To do this, look for a hyperlink on the search engine's page that refers to "Help" or "Instructions." Most search engines, for example, require that you enclose a phrase or term that has spaces in it, like "state tax forms," in quotes. Otherwise, the search engine will not know to match the phrase exactly. Other search engines have a drop-down list box or button that lets you specify this.

Keeping a List of Favorite Web Pages

You can add a web page address to a special folder of favorite web pages, called the **Favorites** folder. By designating a web page as a favorite, you can easily access it in the future without needing to type its URL. This is especially useful for web pages you frequently visit that have long URLs.

To make a web page a favorite, first open the web page. Then choose the Favorites menu's Add To Favorites command, and click OK in the Add Favorite dialog box (see Figure 8-14). To view the web page later, choose the web page from the Favorites bar or the Favorites menu.

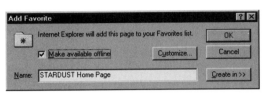

FIGURE 8-14

The Add Favorite dialog box.

Viewing a History Log of Web Pages You've Visited

When you click the History toolbar button, Windows opens a new pane in the Internet Explorer browser window that lists the web sites you've visited in the past 20 days (see Figure 8-15). To see the web sites you visited during a particular week or day, click the week or day in the History bar. To return to one of the web sites, click its entry in this list.

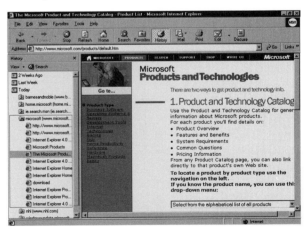

FIGURE 8-15

The History bar shows a record of the web pages you've recently viewed.

To close the History bar, click its Close button.

 To delete a web page listed in the History bar, right-click it and then choose the shortcut menu's Delete command.

If you want to erase your history log, follow these steps:

1 Choose the Tools menu's Internet Options command to display the Internet Options dialog box, as shown in Figure 8-16.

2 Click Clear History.

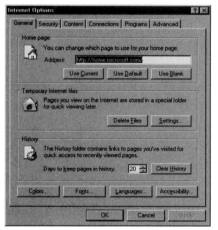

FIGURE 8-16

The Internet Options dialog box.

Printing and Saving a Web Page

You can print and save the web pages you view. To print a web page, click the Print toolbar button. When Windows displays the Print dialog box, use it to describe how you want the web page printed.

 Chapter 2 describes the steps involved in printing. You print web pages in the same manner as you print other files.

To save a web page, choose the File menu's Save As command. When Windows displays the Save As dialog box, use it to name the web page file and specify where you want the file saved.

Notes *Chapter 1 describes how to save files. You save web pages in the same manner as you save other files.*

Working with Channels and Offline Pages

One of the principal problems of using the Web is that it can be awfully slow. If you've visited even a handful of web pages, you already know that you can spend a lot of your time waiting for Internet Explorer to retrieve a web page from some web server.

To address this problem, Internet Explorer 5 provides a couple of handy tools: channels and offline pages. A channel, or channel site, is a special web site that automatically delivers web pages to your desktop. An offline page is a web page that Internet Explorer automatically retrieves or checks for you so you can view it while you're not connected to the Internet (in other words, while you're offline). Typically, you would tell Internet Explorer to retrieve a web page either by clicking a hyperlink or by entering a web page address in the Address box, but with channels and offline pages, you get the web page automatically. You don't have to do anything.

Setting Up Offline Pages

To make a page available for offline viewing, follow these steps:

1 While viewing the web page, choose the Favorites menu's Add To Favorites command to display the Add Favorite dialog box, as shown in Figure 8-17.

FIGURE 8-17

The Add Favorite dialog box.

2 Select the Make Available Offline check box.

3 Click OK to complete the setup process and to **synchronize** your computer with the web page.

Click Customize to create a schedule of times to synchronize your subscribed web page.

Synchronizing Your Offline Pages

To synchronize your offline pages, choose the Tools menu's Synchronize command. Select the check box next to the items you want to synchronize, and then click Synchronize, as shown in Figure 8-18.

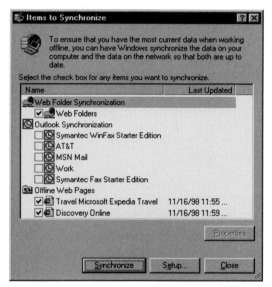

FIGURE 8-18

The Items To Synchronize dialog box.

Viewing Pages Offline

To view synchronized offline pages while not connected to the Internet, choose the File menu's Work Offline command. This disconnects your computer from the Internet until you select a page that is not synchronized. Choose the synchronized page you want to view by selecting a page with a red pushpin that is not "grayed out" from the Favorites bar or the Favorites menu.

 The pages without the red pushpins are your regular favorites, not offline pages. If some regular favorites are not grayed out, it means you have visited them recently and Internet Explorer has saved a local copy of them on your computer (in what is called a cache). You can display the local copy by clicking the page.

Scheduling Subscription Updates

If you want to specify the schedule that Windows uses to update a web page subscription, follow these steps:

1 Choose the Tools menu's Synchronize command to display the Items To Synchronize dialog box.

2 Click Setup to display the Synchronization Settings dialog box.

3 Click the Scheduled tab, and then click Add. This starts the Scheduled Synchronization Wizard. Click Edit to edit an existing schedule.

4 Click Next, and then select your network connection from the drop-down list box.

5 Select the check boxes for the pages you want to update, as shown in Figure 8-19.

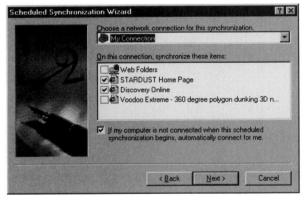

FIGURE 8-19

A screen from the Scheduled Synchronization Wizard.

6 Click Next, and then select when to perform the synchronization.

7 Click Next, and then name your schedule.

8 Click Next, and click Finish.

9 Click OK to close the Synchronization Settings dialog box.

10 Click Synchronize to synchronize your web pages immediately, or click Close to close the Items To Synchronize dialog box.

Canceling Offline Pages

To turn off the offline access to a web page, follow these steps:

1 Choose the Favorites menu's Organize Favorites command.

2 Right-click the web page you want to cancel, and remove the check mark from the Make Available Offline option by clicking it, as shown in Figure 8-20.

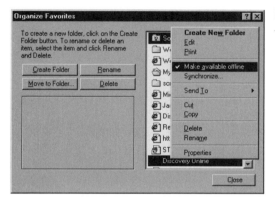

FIGURE 8-20

The Organize Favorites dialog box.

3 Click Close.

Subscribing to a Channel

To subscribe to a channel, follow these steps:

1 Click the Favorites toolbar button, and click Channels on the Favorites bar.

2 Click the channel button that describes the content category you're interested in. For example, if you want to see a travel web site, click the Lifestyle And Travel button. Internet Explorer expands the bar to show the top channels available under that category, as shown in Figure 8-21.

8

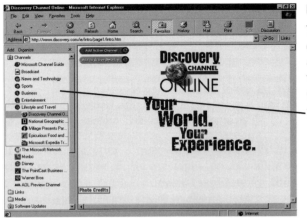

FIGURE 8-21

The Channel bar lists categories of channel sites and specific channels within the selected category.

The Channel bar.

3 Click a channel site to preview the channel.

4 Click the Add Active Channel button to subscribe to the channel.

 To see a longer list of channels available in a category, click the Microsoft Channel Guide button.

CHAPTER 9

Using PowerPoint

Microsoft PowerPoint 2000 is the Office **program** you use to create **presentations.** A presentation is actually a collection of **slides.** These slides can be the kind you view using a projector, but in PowerPoint a slide is an image that you can also view electronically with your computer, print on a transparency and view with an overhead projector, print on paper and distribute, or even save as an **HTML** file and view with a **web browser.**

PowerPoint is an easy program to learn and to use, and once you are familiar with how it works, you might find all sorts of applications for it. This chapter walks you through the processes for doing the following:

- Creating a PowerPoint presentation
- Adding text and pictures
- Formatting slides
- Running a slide show
- Preparing handouts and printing

Creating a PowerPoint Presentation

You can create a PowerPoint presentation in three ways: using the **AutoContent Wizard,** using a **design template,** or using an **AutoLayout.** When you start PowerPoint, you can choose a method in the PowerPoint **dialog box,** as shown in Figure 9-1.

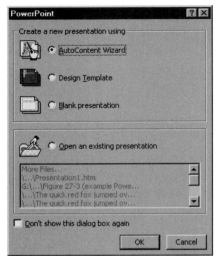

FIGURE 9-1

The opening PowerPoint dialog box.

No particular method is better than the others; which you use depends on what you want to do and how adept you are at working with PowerPoint. The easiest way to create a presentation, however, is to use the AutoContent Wizard, and that's what we'll look at first.

Using the AutoContent Wizard

As do the other Office **wizards,** the AutoContent Wizard asks you a series of questions and then creates a **document** based on your answers. The AutoContent Wizard supplies a design and placeholder content to help you with the appearance and the text of your presentation. To start the AutoContent Wizard, **click** the AutoContent Wizard option button in the opening PowerPoint dialog box, click OK, and follow these steps:

1 Click Next to open the Presentation Type screen.

2 Click a category button to display a list of presentation topics. Figure 9-2 shows the Corporate category and the Employee Orientation topic selected.

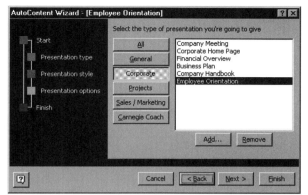

FIGURE 9-2

Select a category and a topic in the Presentation Type screen.

3 Click Next to open the Presentation Style screen, which you use to select the type of output your presentation will use: onscreen, Web, overhead, or 35mm slides. Click an option button, and then click Next.

4 In the Presentation Title box, enter a title for your presentation, and if you want to include footer information on each slide, enter that information in the bottom part of the screen. Clear the Date Last Updated and Slide Number check boxes if you don't want that information displayed on your slides.

5 Click Next, and then click Finish.

6 Choose the File **menu's** Save As command to save the presentation you've just created.

Figure 9-3 shows the employee orientation presentation I created using the AutoContent Wizard. The later section "Adding Text and Pictures" steps you through what you do next in creating a presentation.

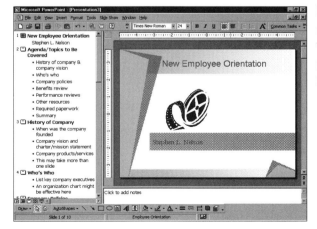

FIGURE 9-3

Use the AutoContent Wizard to easily develop a professional-looking presentation.

Using a Design Template

The quickest way to create a presentation is not with the AutoContent Wizard but with a design template. Click the Design Template option button in the opening PowerPoint dialog box to display the New Presentation dialog box with the Design Templates tab selected, as shown in Figure 9-4.

FIGURE 9-4

Use a design template to quickly develop a new presentation.

To create a presentation using a design template, follow these steps:

1   Browse the list of templates by selecting one to see how it looks in the Preview pane.

2   Select a design template and click OK to display the New Slide dialog box, as shown in Figure 9-5.

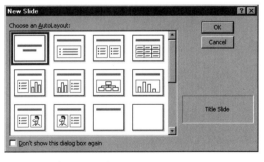

FIGURE 9-5

Select a layout for your new presentation.

3   When you're creating a new presentation, you probably want to start with the first slide, so in the New Slide dialog box, click the first AutoLayout (the Title Slide), and click OK.

Your presentation opens in Normal **view**, and you can now add text and **objects.** Figure 9-6 shows a new presentation created from a design template. The later section "Adding Text and Pictures" explains views and goes through the next steps in creating a presentation.

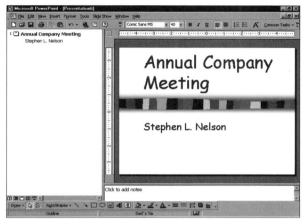

FIGURE 9-6

A new presentation created from a design template.

Instead of choosing a design template in the New Presentation dialog box, you can choose a presentation type from the Presentations tab. Presentation types include content placeholders as well as a design template. The presentation types are the same as those you see in the AutoContent Wizard.

Using a Blank Presentation

When you click the Blank Presentation option button in the opening PowerPoint dialog box and click OK, the next thing you see is the New Slide dialog box, as shown in Figure 9-5. Select an AutoLayout, and click OK to open your presentation in Normal view.

Adding Text and Pictures

Regardless of the way you create a presentation, you add text and pictures in the same way. But before we get into that, I need to mention that PowerPoint displays your presentation in five ways called views: Normal, Outline, Slide, Slide Sorter, and Slide Show. To select a view, click one of the view buttons, as shown in Figure 9-7, which shows a slide in Normal view. Figures 9-8 through 9-11 show how the same slide looks in the other views.

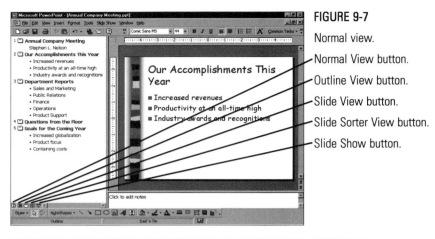

FIGURE 9-7

Normal view.

Normal View button.

Outline View button.

Slide View button.

Slide Sorter View button.

Slide Show button.

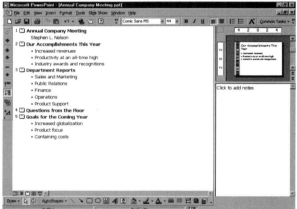

FIGURE 9-8

Outline view.

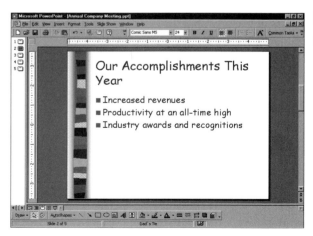

FIGURE 9-9

Slide view.

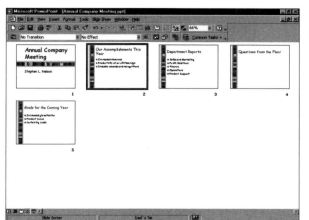

FIGURE 9-10

Slide Sorter view.

FIGURE 9-11

Slide Show view.

Working with PowerPoint Views

Which view you use depends on what you want to do:

- In Normal view, presentation text appears in the pane on the left, and the slide appears in the main pane on the right. You can edit in either pane. You can also add speaker notes in the pane below the main pane. To display a slide in the pane on the right, click its topic in the pane on the left.

- In Outline view, presentation text appears in the main pane on the left, and the slide appears in miniature in the pane on the right. Outline view is best for adding text and speaker notes. You can edit the slide, but doing so is tricky because of its small size. To display the Outlining **toolbar**, right-click a toolbar and choose Outlining. To display a slide in the pane on the right, click its topic in the outline.

- In Slide view, you work with one slide at a time. Click a slide's icon in the left pane to display it in the right pane. Some people prefer to do all their work in Slide view. Because it's larger, you can add or edit text and insert objects and immediately see the effect.

- In Slide Sorter view, you see multiple slides simultaneously. You use Slide Sorter view when you want to change the order of the slides, delete slides, and add special effects such as **animation.** (The later section "Adding Transitions and Animations" explains how to enhance a presentation with animation.)

- In Slide Show view, you see your slides just as they will appear when you run a slide show, that is, in full-screen view. To leave Slide Show view, press the Esc key.

 Speaker notes are notes to yourself about items you might want to mention or information that will serve as a reminder while you're giving a presentation. Your audience can't see speaker notes.

 *The Outlining toolbar in PowerPoint works in exactly the same way as the Outlining toolbar in **Microsoft Word 2000**. Chapter 4 describes the Outlining toolbar.*

Entering and Editing Text

In the early stages of developing a presentation, you'll probably want to work in either Normal view or Outline view. Notice that when you edit text in the text pane, it also changes in the slide.

If you created a presentation using the AutoContent Wizard, your first task is to substitute your text for the placeholder text. To do so, select the text and then type your text. You select text in PowerPoint just as you do in other Office programs. (For a review, see Chapter 2.)

When you are working in the text pane in Normal view or Outline view, you can display the Outlining toolbar and use it to promote and demote headings and sections and to move text up or down just as you do in Word.

To enter or edit text in a slide, you want to work in Normal view or in Slide view. In a slide, text is in a **text box.** To select the text, click to display the text box with its hashed border and sizing handles. You can now edit text and move and size the text box just as you do in Word. (For a review of text boxes, see Chapter 4.) Before you can insert text on a blank slide, you need to insert a text box. Choose the Insert menu's Text Box command, and then enter text as you would in a text box in Word.

Inserting Pictures

The easiest way to see how to add a picture to a slide is to first select an AutoLayout that includes a picture object. To do this, follow these steps:

1 Choose the File menu's New command to display the New Presentation dialog box.

2 In the General tab, select Blank Presentation and click OK to display the New Slide dialog box.

3 Select the first slide on the third row, the Text & Clip Art AutoLayout, and click OK. The slide opens in Normal view, as shown in Figure 9-12.

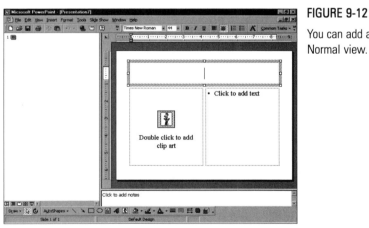

FIGURE 9-12

You can add a picture in Normal view.

4 **Double-click** the picture placeholder to open the Microsoft Clip Gallery dialog box, as shown in Figure 9-13.

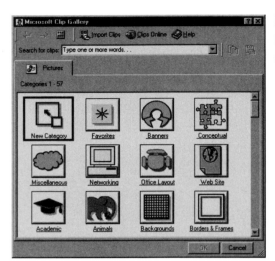

FIGURE 9-13

Use this dialog box to select a picture clip.

5 Click a category icon, browse to select a picture, and then click it to open a pop-up shortcut menu.

6 Click Insert Clip to insert the picture in your document.

When you insert a picture, Word adds the Picture toolbar to the **program window.** You can use its buttons to edit the image. You can also use the **ClipArt Gallery** to add a sound clip or a movie clip to your slide.

Another way to insert a picture or another object in a slide is to choose the Insert menu's Picture command. You'll see the Picture submenu, as shown in Figure 9-14. In addition to inserting a picture, sound clip, or movie clip from the ClipArt Gallery, you can insert a graphics **file,** an AutoShape, an **organization chart, WordArt,** a scanner or camera file, and a **table.**

FIGURE 9-14

Choose the type of "picture" from the submenu.

You can also insert an object created by another program in a PowerPoint slide. For example, to insert a **Microsoft Excel 2000** *worksheet, choose the Insert menu's Object command, and in the Insert Object dialog box, choose Microsoft Excel Worksheet. A worksheet opens in your slide, and the Excel toolbar replaces the PowerPoint toolbar. You can now enter data in the worksheet just as if you had opened Excel.*

Formatting Slides

Whether you create a slide from scratch, use the AutoContent Wizard to create a presentation, or select a design template or a presentation, you can customize any slide. You can change the **font** style and type, choose different colors, use a different scheme for bulleted and numbered lists, and so on.

 Always be aware of presentation output when formatting slides. For example, light text against a dark background can be difficult to read on the printed page, but it looks great on the screen.

Formatting Text

You can format text on a slide using all the usual Office formatting tools, but you have some text formatting tools that are unique to PowerPoint:

- The Replace Fonts command
- The Increase Font Size toolbar button
- The Decrease Font Size toolbar button

When you use the Replace Fonts command, you replace all instances of one font in a presentation with another font. To replace one font with another font, follow these steps:

1 Choose the Format menu's Replace Fonts command to display the Replace Font dialog box, as shown in Figure 9-15.

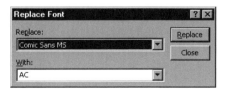

FIGURE 9-15

Replace one font with another in the presentation using the Replace Font dialog box.

2 If necessary, enter the name of the font you want to replace in the Replace box, or select a font from the drop-down list.

3 Click the With drop-down arrow to select a substitute font.

4 Click Replace.

You can change the size of selected text by clicking the Font Size toolbar button and selecting a size or by typing a size in the Font Size box and pressing the Enter key. But you can also increase or decrease the font size in a more general way. To do this, follow these steps:

1 Select the text for which you want to change font size.

2 Click the Increase Font Size toolbar button or the Decrease Font Size toolbar button to change the font size in standard increments.

 Notes *When you use the Increase Font Size and Decrease Font Size toolbar buttons, the size changes according to the increments in the Font Size drop-down list.*

In addition to formatting the font and font size, you can enhance selected text with a shadow, color, and alignment. To add a shadow to selected text, click the Text Shadow toolbar button. To change the color of selected text, click the Font Color drop-down arrow on the Drawing toolbar, and select a color. To change the alignment of selected text, click one of the alignment toolbar buttons. You can center text, justify it, left-align it, or right-align it, just as you do in Word.

Working with Color

The easiest way to work with color in your slides is to use a design template and then modify it. Professionals in the graphic arts field selected the color schemes in PowerPoint's design templates, so you'll probably want to think twice about changing them. That said, there are some very good reasons for changing color schemes. For example, you might want to use a particular design template for printed output that has a dark background and light text. In this case, you'll need to change the background from dark to light and probably change the light text to dark.

To change a color scheme, follow these steps:

1 Open the presentation, and choose the Format menu's Slide Color Scheme command to display the Color Scheme dialog box, as shown in Figure 9-16.

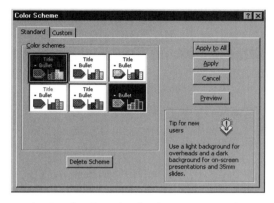

FIGURE 9-16

The Standard tab in the Color Scheme dialog box.

2 In the Standard tab, you can select one of the preformatted color schemes. To use it for a single slide (the one that is open in the active presentation), click Apply. To use it for all slides in a presentation, click Apply to All.

3 If none of the preformatted color schemes appeals to you, click the Custom tab, as shown in Figure 9-17, to create your own.

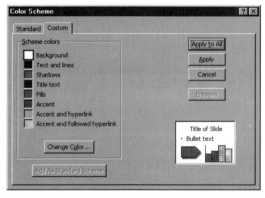

FIGURE 9-17

Creating a custom color scheme.

4 Click the color you want to change, and then click Change Color to display the Color dialog box.

5 Use the color palette in the Standard tab to select a color, or click the Custom tab to mix your own colors. When you're finished, click OK.

6 In the Color Scheme dialog box, click Apply or Apply To All.

You can change the background color of a slide in the Custom tab of the Color Scheme dialog box, but if you want to change a background graphic as well, you'll need to do so in the Background dialog box. To do this, follow these steps:

1 Choose the Format menu's Background command to display the Background dialog box, as shown in Figure 9-18.

FIGURE 9-18

Use this dialog box to delete a background graphic.

2 Select the Omit Background Graphics From Master check box to delete the graphic.

3 To change the background color, use the Background Fill drop-down list.

4 Click Apply or Apply to All.

Changing the Layout and the Design Template

You can easily change the layout of a slide. For example, if you've chosen a bulleted list layout and find that you really need two-column text, click the Common Tasks button, choose Slide Layout to display the Slide Layout dialog box, select the 2 Column Text AutoLayout, and click Reapply. PowerPoint applies the new format to your slide.

Just as easily you can change the design template for a presentation. Open the presentation, click the Common Tasks toolbar button, and select Apply Design Template to display the Apply Design Template dialog box, as shown in Figure 9-19.

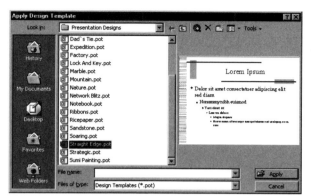

FIGURE 9-19

The Apply Design
Template dialog box.

Select a new design template, and click Apply. PowerPoint applies the
new design to all slides in the presentation.

Modifying the Slide Master

As you have seen, you can change the color scheme, background, or
design template and apply it to all the slides in a presentation. When
you want to make other changes and apply them to all slides in a
presentation, you use the Slide Master. For example, if you want all
slides in a presentation to include your company logo, insert it on the
Slide Master. Most designs include a master for the title slide and a
master for the other slides in a presentation.

To open the Slide Master, choose the View menu's Master command and
the submenu's Slide Master command. You'll see something similar to
Figure 9-20. To edit any text box, click it. You can format text in all the
usual ways, and you can move or delete placeholders for graphic objects
and text boxes.

FIGURE 9-20

The Slide Master.

You can also use the Slide Master to enter footer information—the date, the slide number, and other text. To enter footer information, follow these steps:

1 Choose the View menu's Header And Footer command to display the Header And Footer dialog box, as shown in Figure 9-21.

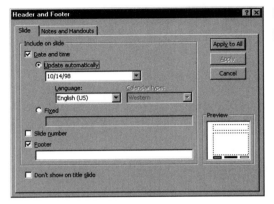

FIGURE 9-21

Entering footer information.

2 If necessary, click the Slide tab.

3 If you want the date and time to update automatically every time you open the presentation, select the Date And Time check box, and then click the Update Automatically option button. If you want to insert a date that remains the same whenever you open the presentation, click the Fixed option button and enter a date in the drop-down list box.

4 If you want the slide number to appear in the footer, select the Slide Number check box.

5 To display other information in the footer (which will appear centered unless you move the text box on the Slide Master), select the Footer check box and enter the information (this can be text and/or a graphic) in the box.

6 Select the Don't Show On Title Slide if you don't want the footer information to display on the title slide.

7 When you're finished, click Apply To All. (The Apply option is not available if you open the Header And Footer dialog box from the Slide Master as we've done here.)

Adding Transitions and Animations

A **transition** is a special effect that occurs when a slide first appears on the screen—for example, a bulleted list dropping down from the top. Transition effects occur between slides. You add transitions in Slide Sorter view, using the options in the Slide Transition Effects drop-down list. After you add a transition to a slide, a transition icon appears below and to the left of the slide.

To customize the speed of the transition and, perhaps, to add sound, follow these steps:

1 Select the slide, and then click the Slide Transition toolbar button to display the Slide Transition dialog box, as shown in Figure 9-22.

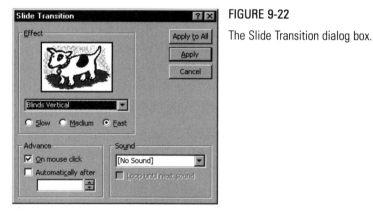

FIGURE 9-22

The Slide Transition dialog box.

2 Select an effect and its speed.

3 Specify whether you want slides to advance automatically or when you click the mouse, and select a sound if you want.

4 Click Apply or Apply To All.

An **animation** is a special effect that occurs within a slide—for example, bulleted items appearing one at a time. To animate text, use Slide Sorter view and select an animation from the Present Animation drop-down list. To animate a graphic, follow these steps:

1 In Slide Sorter view, double-click a slide to open it in Normal view.

2 Right-click a toolbar, and choose the shortcut menu's Animation Effects command to display the Animation Effects toolbar.

3 Select the graphic, and then select an animation effect from the toolbar.

4 To see the results of the animation effect, switch back to Slide Sorter view, select the slide, and click the Animation Effect icon that has been added below the slide.

Running a Slide Show

You can run a slide show automatically or manually. If you create a presentation for a kiosk or for a booth at a trade show, for example, the presentation should run automatically, and you'll need to set the timing. If you'll be using your slide show to augment a spoken presentation, you'll probably run the slide show manually.

Timing Your Presentation

When you're timing your presentation, be sure that you allow a viewer enough time to read everything that's on a slide and to see any graphics long enough to understand their importance. To set up automatic timings, follow these steps:

1 Open your presentation in Slide Sorter view, and click the Rehearse Timings toolbar button. Your presentation opens in Slide view, and the Rehearsal dialog box is displayed at the top of the screen, as shown in Figure 9-23.

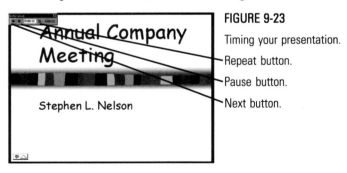

FIGURE 9-23

Timing your presentation.

Repeat button.

Pause button.

Next button.

 A good way to determine how long a slide should appear on the screen is to read its contents aloud.

2   Click Next to advance through the slides.

 The numbers in the middle of the Rehearsal dialog box indicate the time for the current slide. The numbers at the right side indicate the total time elapsed for the presentation.

3   When you finish the rehearsal, choose Yes to record the timings and use them when you run the slide show.

Setting Up Your Presentation

Whether you'll be running your presentation automatically or manually, you have one more task to take care of before you begin. To set up a slide show, follow these steps:

1   Choose the Slide Show menu's Set Up Show command to display the Set Up Show dialog box, as shown in Figure 9-24.

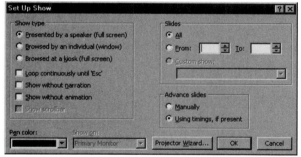

FIGURE 9-24

Setting up a slide show.

2   In the Show Type section, select the presentation method.

3   In the Slides section, specify whether to show all the slides or only a selection.

4   In the Advance Slides section, specify automatic or manual presentation.

5   Choose a pen color you'll use to draw on the screen during the presentation.

6   Click OK.

 If you'll be running your slide show using a data projector connected to your computer, click Projector Wizard to set up the data projector.

When you click on the last slide in a slide show presentation, you return to PowerPoint. To end on a black slide, choose the Tools menu's Options command, and in the Options dialog box, click the View tab and select the End With Black Slide check box.

Running Your Presentation

At last, you're ready to run your slide show! Choose the Slide Show menu's View Show command. If you're running a manual presentation, simply click the mouse to advance to the next slide. As you can see in Figure 9-25, PowerPoint adds a shortcut menu button in the lower left corner of the screen. During a presentation, you can click this button to display a menu from which you can choose to black the screen, display speaker notes, select a pen color and draw on the screen, and open the Meeting Minder to take notes. Figure 9-26 shows this shortcut menu.

FIGURE 9-25

Running a slide show.

FIGURE 9-26

The shortcut menu you can use while running a slide show.

If you want to take notes during the presentation, open the shortcut menu and choose Meeting Minder, as shown in Figure 9-27. Use the Meeting Minutes tab to enter notes, and use the Action Items tab to create a to-do list, complete with a date and the name of the person responsible for the action item.

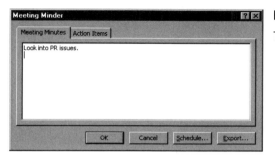

FIGURE 9-27

The Meeting Minder dialog box.

 To give a presentation using Microsoft NetMeeting, choose the Tools menu's Online Collaboration command and choose a command from the submenu to meet or schedule a meeting.

Preparing Handouts and Printing

If you've been to many conferences or seminars that include slide shows, you're familiar with printed handouts. In PowerPoint, you can create handouts of your slides or your outline. To prepare a handout, use the Handout Master, and follow these steps:

1 With your presentation open, choose the View menu's Master command and the submenu's Handout Master command.

2 If necessary, right-click any toolbar and choose the shortcut menu's Handout Master command to display the Handout Master toolbar, as shown in Figure 9-28.

9

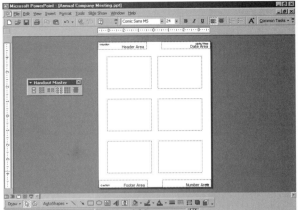

FIGURE 9-28

Preparing a Handout
Master.

3 Click a button on the Handout Master toolbar to specify how many slides to print on a page or to print your outline. (Point to a button to display its name.)

To print handouts, slides, notes pages, or Outline view, choose the File menu's Print command to display the Print dialog box, as shown in Figure 9-29. The first two sections of the Print dialog box are similar to the Print dialog box you see in any Office program. (If you have questions about the options in the first two sections, refer to Chapter 2.) The third section contains options that are specific to PowerPoint.

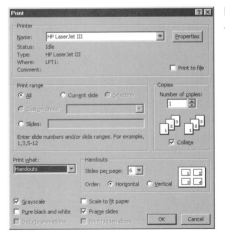

FIGURE 9-29

The Print dialog box.

In the Print What drop-down list, specify what you want to print. If you select Handouts, use the Handouts section to specify the number of slides per page and whether you want the slides laid out vertically or horizontally.

If your slides use color and you'll be using a noncolor printer, select the Grayscale check box to optimize the appearance of color. If you want to print faster, select the Pure Black And White check box. This changes all shades of gray to either black or white.

If the slides themselves don't include a border, select the Frame Slides check box. You'll almost always want to do this.

When you've specified all the options, click OK to print.

CHAPTER 10

Introducing Publisher

With **Microsoft Publisher 2000,** you can quickly and easily create well-designed common publications such as newsletters, brochures, flyers, signs, banners, postcards, letterhead, envelopes, and business cards. You can then print the publications you create on your own printer, or you can prepare them for professional printing. In this chapter I walk you through the steps involved in creating a publication with Publisher by discussing the following topics:

- Creating a new publication using a **wizard**
- Getting acquainted with Publisher and its tools
- Adding content to a publication
- Printing your publication

Creating a New Publication Using a Wizard

Publisher comes with several wizards that make creating publications a snap. When you use a wizard to create a publication, all you need to do is fill in the content blanks—the wizard designs the layout for you. The steps of the wizard differ depending on the type of publication you're creating, but the process is much the same for all. I'll use the **Web Site** Wizard in the following example. To work with a wizard, follow these steps:

1 When you start Publisher, the **program** automatically displays the Catalog window, as shown in Figure 10-1. Or if you have a publication open and you want to create a new one using a wizard, choose the File **menu's** New command to display the Catalog window.

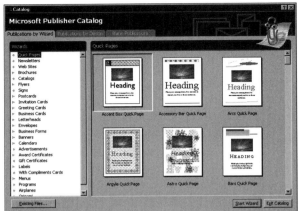

FIGURE 10-1

The Microsoft Publisher Catalog.

Notes   *To browse through Publisher's wizards by **design template** rather than by type of publication, **click** the Publications By Design tab. To create a new publication from scratch, click the Blank Publications tab.*

2   Select the type of publication you want to create from the Wizards list on the left pane. To create a web site, for example, select Web Sites. If you select a type that has an arrow next to it, the list expands to show the content categories available for that type. Select a category from within the type.

Notes   *Some of Publisher's publications have two categories: Plain Paper and Special Paper. The Special Paper category includes designs specially created for printing on preprinted paper from Paper Direct, a direct mail paper supplier.*

3   Select a design for the publication by clicking a picture in the list on the right pane.

The better a design fits the type and amount of content you want to include, the less work it means for you. So select a design carefully. Usually, the more specific you are when describing your type of publication, the better the design suits your publication. But this isn't always the case. Don't feel confined to using only the designs listed under your type of publication. Check out the designs for other types of publications if you can't find a good fit.

4   Click Start Wizard to start the wizard for the design you selected.

5 The first time you go through a wizard, Publisher prompts you to fill in some information about yourself. Click OK to display the Personal Information **dialog box** shown in Figure 10-2.

6 Select an information set from the top list box and enter the information for that set. Click Update when you're done filling in the information for all sets that apply to you. Publisher saves the information you enter, so you don't have to reenter it for future publications you create.

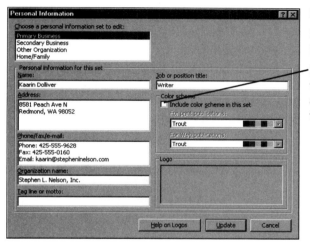

FIGURE 10-2

Entering personal information.

Select this check box to use the same color scheme in all publications you create for this set of information.

7 Publisher creates and displays the publication (in this example, a web site) and displays the wizard on the left side of the window, as shown in Figure 10-3.

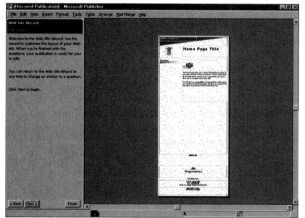

FIGURE 10-3

The beginnings of a new publication.

8 Click Next to start the wizard.

Publisher assumes that you want to use the wizard to guide you through the process of creating the publication. If you click outside the wizard while you're creating the publication, Publisher reminds you that the wizard is there to help you. To skip past the wizard's questions and begin editing the publication immediately, click Finish.

9 The Web Site Wizard, like most wizards, first asks which color scheme you want to use for the web site. Select a set of colors from the list it displays, as shown in Figure 10-4. When you click a set, Publisher changes the publication to reflect the color scheme you selected. Click different color schemes until you find the one you want. Then click Next.

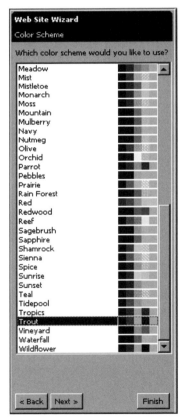

FIGURE 10-4

Selecting a color scheme.

If you won't print your publication in color, select the Black & Gray color scheme. This way you can be sure that what you see on the screen will be readable and attractive when printed.

For many publications, the wizard asks about the paper size and orientation you'll use for the publication. The choices differ depending on the type of publication you're creating.

10 The wizard asks which predesigned pages you want to include, as shown in Figure 10-5. Select the check boxes next to the pages you want in the web site. As you do this, Publisher adds the pages to the site. Click Next to continue.

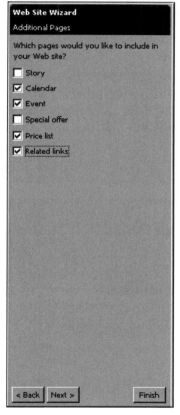

FIGURE 10-5

Adding pages to the web site.

11 The wizard asks whether you want to add a form to your web site for visitors to complete and submit. If you want to include a form in your web site, click one of the form option buttons. When you do so, Publisher adds the form and tells you which page it's on. Click OK. If you don't want to include a form, click None.

12 Click Next. The wizard asks whether you want to include a navigation bar on the pages of your web site. The navigation bar contains a series of buttons that link to the other pages in the web site. It's a useful tool that allows visitors to quickly navigate your web site.

13 Click Next. The wizard asks whether you want the home page to play a sound. Sound **files** tend to be large, so you might not want to use sound. The **web page** might take too long to load.

14 Click Next. Tell the wizard whether you want to use the design's background texture. You can try it and then turn it off later if it hinders the legibility of the text. Click Finish.

15 The Web Site Wizard, like most other wizards, lastly asks which set of personal information you want to use in the publication. Select an information set. Click Update if you need to fill out, review, or edit the set.

16 Click Finish.

After you finish creating a publication using a wizard, Publisher displays the publication for you to edit, as described in the next section. However, the wizard stays along the left pane of the publication so you can easily change any settings. The wizard might also have new options you can use to edit the publication.

Getting Acquainted with Publisher and Its Tools

Publisher contains all the cool tools you need to create and customize professional-looking publications in a snap. Publisher isn't a tricky program, but if you've never used it before, you might be a bit bewildered by the look of it and the options it provides. This section familiarizes you with the layout of the Publisher **program window** and describes how you move around in Publisher and use tools unique to the program.

A Quick Look at the Publisher Window

This section familiarizes you with the layout of Publisher, as shown in Figure 10-6. Getting the feel for Publisher's layout makes moving around in Publisher and editing **objects** much easier.

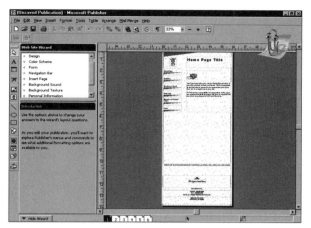

FIGURE 10-6

The Publisher program
window.

The wizard appears in the left pane of the program window. To hide the
wizard so you have more room to view your publication, click the Hide
Wizard button located at the bottom of the wizard. The wizard disap-
pears, as shown in Figure 10-7. To get the wizard back, click Show
Wizard.

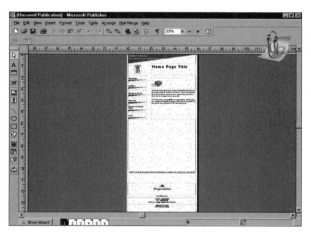

FIGURE 10-7

The Publisher program
window without the wizard.

In the right pane of the program window is the publication you're
creating (see Figure 10-6). At the bottom of the window, you can see the
numbered pages of the publication. If the publication contains more
than one page, click a different page to display that page.

Zooming

In order to see what you're working on in your publication, you need to zoom in on it. Publisher provides several ways in which you can refocus on the area you're working on:

- The Zoom button on the Standard **toolbar** allows you to specify the size of the publication as viewed on the screen as a percentage of its actual size.

- The Zoom In and Zoom Out buttons next to the Zoom button allow you to zoom in and out on the selected **frame,** or, if no frame is selected, on the portion of the publication currently displayed in the middle of the window.

- Right-click the publication, and choose the shortcut menu's Whole Page command to view an entire page of the publication at once in the Publisher window.

- Press the F9 key to toggle the **view** between actual size, as shown in Figure 10-8, and the view used before pressing F9.

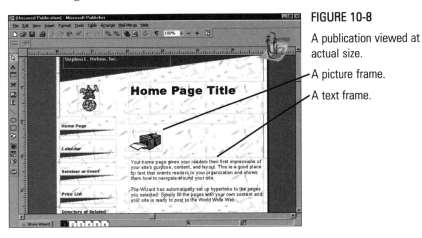

FIGURE 10-8

A publication viewed at actual size.

A picture frame.

A text frame.

Working with Frames

Before you begin editing, your publication will probably contain several elements: text placeholders, picture placeholders, and perhaps place-holders for a logo or other object, such as a mailing address. These elements all have gray boxes around them, which Publisher calls frames. Here's a sampling of what you can do with Publisher's frames:

- Select a frame by clicking within it. You can tell which frame is selected because Publisher adds handles to the edges of the frame, as shown in Figure 10-9.

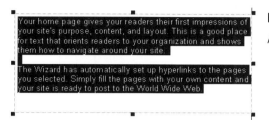

FIGURE 10-9

A selected text frame.

- Zoom in on a frame by right-clicking it and choosing the shortcut menu's Selected Object command.
- Resize a frame by selecting the frame and pointing to one of the frame's handles until the pointer turns into the Resize pointer. Then **drag** the handle inward or outward to make the frame smaller or larger.
- Move a frame by selecting the frame and pointing to an edge of the frame until the mouse pointer turns into the Move pointer. Then drag the frame to a new location.

 If you notice one or more colored boxes within a frame you have selected, it means the frame contains multiple objects grouped together. To move or work with the objects individually, you must first ungroup them either by clicking the Ungroup Objects button (which looks like two connected puzzle pieces) at the bottom of the frame or by choosing the Arrange menu's Ungroup Objects command.

Working with Publisher's Toolbars

The Standard and Formatting toolbars run across the top of the Publisher window, just as in the other Office programs. These toolbars, shown in Figure 10-10, consist primarily of the buttons you're familiar with from the Standard and Formatting toolbars of the other Office programs, but they also contain a few extra drawing tools that usually appear on the Drawing toolbar.

 Unlike the other Office programs, Publisher does not have a Personal toolbar that combines commonly used Standard and Formatting toolbar buttons.

If you select a picture, WordArt, or clip art object, Publisher displays this Formatting toolbar.

FIGURE 10-10

The Standard and Formatting toolbars in Publisher.

The Objects toolbar runs down the left side of the Publisher window (see Figure 10-8). It contains several useful tools for working with objects in Publisher, as described in the following table. Table 10-1 describes the Objects toolbar buttons from top to bottom.

Button	Function
Pointer Tool	Lets you select an object.
Text Frame Tool	Lets you create a new text frame.
Table Frame Tool	Lets you create a new **table** frame.
WordArt Frame Tool	Lets you create a new **WordArt** frame.
Picture Frame Tool	Lets you create a new picture frame.
Clip Gallery Tool	Displays the Clip Art Gallery dialog box so you can select a clip art image to insert.
Line Tool	Lets you draw a line.
Oval Tool	Lets you draw an oval. Hold down the Shift key to draw a circle.
Rectangle Tool	Lets you draw a rectangle. Hold down the Shift key to draw a square.
Custom Shapes	Displays a list of shapes that you can insert.
Hot Spot Tool	Lets you select an area of a page or object and turn it into a **hyperlink**.
Form Control	Displays a list of form fields you can add to a web form.
HTML Code Fragment	Displays a dialog box for inserting **HTML** code in a web page.
Design Gallery Object	Displays the Design Gallery dialog box, which you can use to insert predesigned objects typically found in publications.

TABLE 10-1: The Objects toolbar buttons.

Adding Content to a Publication

After you've created the basic design of your publication, you're ready to begin adding content. Publisher lets you add two types of content: text and pictures.

Adding Text

You can add text to a publication in a couple of primary ways: by replacing text in placeholders with your own text or by creating new text frames and filling these frames with text. If the wizard created a placeholder for the text you want to add, you can replace the dummy text with your text by clicking the text frame to highlight the text and then typing your text. If the text you type doesn't fit in the frame, Publisher may decrease the **font** size so it does. You can let Publisher do this if you want to make the text fit, or you can set the font size to the specific size you want and then tell Publisher that you want the text to continue in another text frame. When a frame holds more text than it can display with the current text settings, Publisher displays a little box at the bottom of the frame with the letter A and an ellipses (three dots), as shown in Figure 10-11.

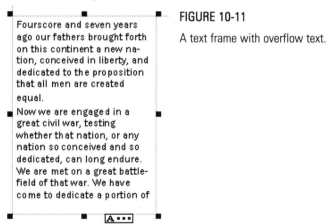

FIGURE 10-11

A text frame with overflow text.

If you want the overflow text to continue into an existing empty text frame, follow these steps:

1 Click the text frame that has too much text to select it.

2 Click the Connect Text Frames button on the Connect Frames toolbar. The mouse pointer turns into a pitcher icon.

3 Click the empty text frame to "pour" the remaining text into that frame.

To move between connected frames (for instance, if they're on different pages), click the Go To Previous Frame and Go To Next Frame buttons on the Connect Frames toolbar. To disconnect connected frames and remove the text from the overflow frame, select the first frame and click the Disconnect Text Frames toolbar button.

To create a new text frame, follow these steps:

1 Click the Text Frame Tool button on the Objects toolbar.

2 Position the pointer where you want one corner of the text frame and drag diagonally to the location where you want the opposite corner. This creates an empty text frame, as shown in Figure 10-12.

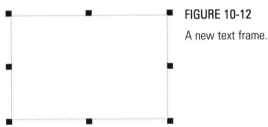

FIGURE 10-12

A new text frame.

3 Begin typing in the text frame.

 To move text between frames without moving the frame itself, select the text you want to move and rest the mouse pointer over the text until the mouse pointer turns into the Drag tool with the letter T. *Then drag the text to another frame. Release the mouse button when Publisher adds a red border around the frame. If you drop the text in an area without a text frame, Publisher creates a new text frame.*

Adding Pictures

Publisher lets you add four types of pictures to your publications: images stored as files, clip art images, drawings, and scanned or captured images. To insert a picture in an existing picture frame, follow these steps:

1 Right-click the frame, and choose the shortcut menu's Change Picture command and the submenu's Picture command.

2 Select the type of picture you want to insert from the Picture submenu, as shown in Figure 10-13.

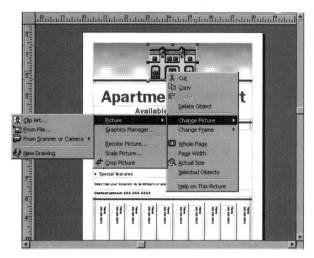

FIGURE 10-13

Choosing a type of picture to insert.

- Choose Clip Art to display the Insert Clip Art window, and select a clip art image to insert.

- Choose From File to display the Insert Picture dialog box and select an image file to insert.

- Choose From Scanner Or Camera and choose Select Device to display the Select Source dialog box and select the camera or scanner you want to use. Then choose the Acquire Image command to display a dialog box for scanning or capturing the image.

- Choose New Drawing to turn the picture frame into a blank canvas and display the Drawing and AutoShapes toolbars.

 If the graphic file you want to insert is large and you want to keep the size of your publication down, you can link to the graphic rather than embedding it in the publication. To add a link to a graphic, right-click the picture placeholder and choose the shortcut menu's Change Picture command. Then choose the Graphics Manager command. In the Graphics Manager dialog box, click Create Link. Click the first option button, and click OK. Use the Link To Graphic dialog box to locate the graphic file to which you want the frame to link. If you later want to change the graphic, display the Graphics Manager dialog box, select the linked graphic, and click Update.

To create a new picture frame, click the Picture Frame Tool button on the Objects toolbar. Position the pointer where you want one corner of the picture frame and drag diagonally to the location where you want the opposite corner. Then add a picture to the new frame as described in the steps above.

Adding WordArt

You can use WordArt to design logos, emphasize text, and generally jazz up a layout. To create a new WordArt frame for your text, click the WordArt Frame Tool button on the Objects toolbar and drag where you want the WordArt object to go. When you do so, Publisher displays the Enter Your Text Here dialog box and replaces the Standard and Formatting toolbars with a WordArt toolbar, as shown in Figure 10-14. Enter your WordArt text in the dialog box, and click Update Display. Then use WordArt's toolbar buttons to customize the WordArt object. Table 10-2 describes what each of the WordArt toolbar buttons does.

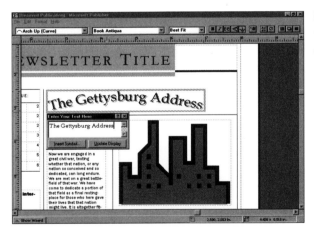

FIGURE 10-14

The Publisher window after you add a WordArt frame.

Button	What It Does
Shape	Displays a selection of WordArt shapes from which you can choose.
Font	Lets you change the font of the WordArt text.
Font Size	Lets you change the font size of the WordArt text.
Bold	Boldfaces the WordArt text.

Button	What It Does
Italic	Italicizes the WordArt text.
Even Height	Makes all letters of the WordArt text the same height, even if some are capitalized and some are lowercase.
Flip Left	Flips the WordArt text on its side.
Stretch	Stretches the WordArt text to fill the frame.
Align	Displays a drop-down menu of choices for aligning the WordArt text in the frame.
Spacing	Displays the Spacing Between Characters dialog box, which you can use to specify the character spacing of the WordArt text.
Adjust	Displays the Special Effects dialog box, which you can use to customize such specifications as the spacing, rotation, or arc of the WordArt text.
Color	Displays the Shading dialog box, which you can use to change the pattern of the WordArt text or the color of the WordArt text or background.
Shadow	Displays the Shadow dialog box, which you can use to select a shadow effect.
Add Border	Displays the Border dialog box, which you can use to select a text border.

TABLE 10-2: The WordArt toolbar buttons.

When you finish creating the WordArt, click anywhere outside the WordArt frame to return to the regular Publisher window.

Adding Design Gallery Objects

Publisher comes with a large collection of elements commonly used in publications, such as advertisements, coupons, and forms to fill out. Publisher saves you the wear and tear of designing these sorts of time-consuming layouts yourself. To add one of these elements to your publication, follow these steps:

1   Click the Design Gallery Object button on the Objects toolbar to display the Design Gallery window, as shown in Figure 10-15.

10

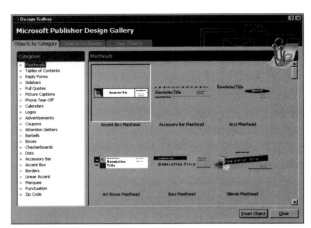

FIGURE 10-15

The Microsoft Publisher Design Gallery.

2   Select an object category from the Categories list.

3   Click a picture in the right pane to select a design for the object.

4   Click Insert Object.

5   Drag the object to the place where you want it, and then resize it or customize it as necessary.

Inserting Mailing Information

Publisher comes with a feature called the Publisher Address List, which you can use to store addresses for use in publications you intend to mail. Let's begin by looking at the Publisher Address List and then seeing how to insert addresses in your publications using Publisher's **Mail Merge** feature.

Notes   *If you already have the mailing information you want to use in a publication stored as a **database** or in your Microsoft Outlook **Contacts** folder, you don't need to use Publisher's Address List feature to enter mailing addresses. Publisher can import the address information from these other programs.*

To create a Publisher Address List, follow these steps:

1   Choose the Mail Merge menu's Create Publisher Address List command to display the New Address List dialog box.

To add or remove fields in the Address List, click Customize.

---

2 Enter information for the first contact, as shown in Figure 10-16.

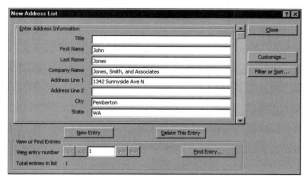

FIGURE 10-16

Creating a new list of mailing addresses.

3 Click New Entry to proceed to the next contact.

4 When you finish entering address information for your first few contacts, click Close to display the Save As dialog box.

5 Name your Address List. For example, you might name your list of business contacts Business Address List or your list of personal contacts Personal Address List.

6 Enter a storage location for the Address List (your My Documents **folder** is probably a good choice), and click Save.

Notes   *To edit or add contacts to an Address List you've saved, choose the Mail Merge menu's Edit Publisher Address List command. Use the View Entry Number buttons to move back and forth through the list.*

To insert mailing information from a **data source** in a publication, follow these steps:

1 If your publication includes a placeholder for an address, select this placeholder. If your publication doesn't include a mailing address placeholder, create a text frame where you want the address information to go.

2 Choose the Mail Merge menu's Open Data Source command.

3 If you're merging from an Outlook Contacts folder, click the arrow button beside the first option. If you're merging from a Publisher Address List or a **Microsoft Access 2000** database, click the arrow beside the second option. If you select the second option, Publisher displays the Open Data Source dialog box.

4 Use the Open Data Source dialog box to locate the address source. When you find it, click Open to display the Insert Fields dialog box.

5 Select the first field, and click Insert. Then add spacing or punctuation, and insert the rest of the fields in the order in which you want them to go, as shown in Figure 10-17.

FIGURE 10-17

Inserting fields from an address list.

The fields look like this when you insert them.

6 When you've inserted all the fields you want to include, click Close to close the Insert Fields dialog box. Then choose the Mail Merge menu's Merge command to display the Preview Data dialog box. Publisher shows you how the first contact's information looks in the mailing address frame, as shown in Figure 10-18.

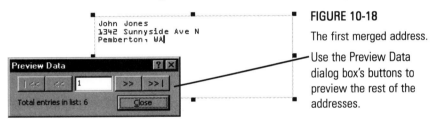

FIGURE 10-18

The first merged address.

Use the Preview Data dialog box's buttons to preview the rest of the addresses.

When a publication includes merged fields, Publisher changes the Print command to the Print Merge command. Use this command to specify the contact entries for which you want to print copies of the publication.

Printing Your Publication

Publisher offers not just one but two printing options: you can print a publication yourself, much as you print other Office documents, or you can use the Pack And Go Wizard to take your publication to a printer for printing. Publisher's commercial printing options simplify the complicated, but relatively common task of taking a publication to a printer.

Printing a Publication Using Your Printer

To print a publication directly, choose the File menu's Print command to display the Print dialog box. You'll recognize most of Publisher's print options from the other Office programs. But when you look closely you'll see that the Print dialog box includes a couple of extra buttons. To print the publication with facing pages on one sheet of paper, click Book Printing Options. To specify how graphics should print, which fonts should be used, whether you want to print printer marks and bleeds, and other such advanced settings, click Advanced Print Settings.

Preparing a Publication for Professional Printing

If you want to print your Publisher publication out-of-house, you use Publisher's Pack And Go Wizard. To use the wizard, follow these steps:

1 Choose the File menu's Pack And Go command and the submenu's Take To A Commercial Printing Service command.

 Notes *The wizard for taking your publication to another computer just contains a subset of the options for taking your publication to a commercial printing service.*

2 Click Next to start the wizard.

3 Select a location for storing the exportable Publisher file. You probably want to store it on a removable medium, such as a **Zip** disk or floppy disk. If you want to use floppy disks, have several blank disks ready.

4 Select the check boxes next to the options you want to include on the disks for the printer (see Figure 10-19). Checked boxes increase the file's size, but unless you're really concerned about file size, you probably want all the boxes checked to minimize the risk of printer error.

- Select the Embed TrueType fonts check box to include the font information in the publication. Normally, a **document** doesn't include font information. If a printer doesn't have the exact same fonts that you used in the publication, the fonts won't print correctly.

- Select the Include Linked Graphics check box to include the graphic files for graphics linked to the publication on the printer's disk.

10

- Select the Create Links For Embedded Graphics check box to link embedded graphics to their original graphic files. This allows the printer to confirm that the publication uses the most recent graphic files.

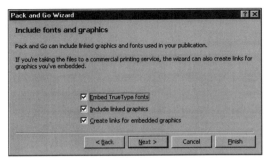

FIGURE 10-19

The Pack And Go Wizard.

5 Click Next.

6 Click Finish.

CHAPTER 11

Introducing Access

Microsoft Access 2000 is a *relational **database*** program. It's a very powerful tool, but it can also be a bit intimidating. In this chapter I introduce Access and describe the basics of working with Access, covering the following topics:

- What is a relational database?
- Using a **wizard** to create a new database
- Adding and updating information in your database
- **Querying** your database
- Reporting on database information

What Is a Relational Database?

Access lets you create relational databases. To learn what a relational database is, let's start with the second part of the term, *database*. A database is simply a collection of information, or data, that's arranged so you can manipulate it in useful ways. For example, you can sort it, or search it, or print mailing labels from it. Most of us use databases every day. Your address book is a database of names, addresses, and phone numbers. So is the phone book. Your checkbook is a database of financial transactions.

Some databases are more complex. When the clerk at the supermarket scans the package of lime Jell-O you're buying, the scanner asks, or queries, the store's database for information about the number (the Universal Product Code) encoded in the package bar code. It then prints the results—product description and price—on your receipt. The scanner also tells the database "We just sold another package of lime Jell-O," so the database can keep track of inventory levels, print sales reports, and so on.

So what's a *relational* database? The easiest way to describe a relational database is by comparing it with the other type of database, a flat database. Suppose you own a video store and you want to design a database to keep track of each video rental—what movie was rented, who you rented it to, and so forth. Suppose you also want the database to be able to do things like print mailing labels, so you can send direct mailers to your customers. And while you're at it, it would be handy if the database could search for movies by director or actor. That way you can help customers when they come to you looking for "this old movie starring Robert Mitchum."

All databases store their data in **tables.** If you've used **Microsoft Word 2000** or **Microsoft Excel 2000** or some other **program** to build tables, a database table is similar. Figure 11-1 shows a flat database.

ID	Title	FirstName	LastName	Phone	Address	City	Zip	Director	Ac
1001	Gone with the Wind	Nancy	Davolio	(425) 555-1234	507 - 20th Ave. E.	Seattle	98122-	Victor Fleming	Clark Ga
1002	Thunderball	Andrew	Fuller	(425) 555-4321	908 W. Capital Way	Tacoma	98401-	Terence Young	Sean Co
1003	Die Hard	Andrew	Fuller	(425) 555-4321	908 W. Capital Way	Tacoma	98401-	John McTiernan	Bruce W
mber)									

FIGURE 11-1

A portion of a flat database table for a video store.

Each row of a database holds one **record** (in this case, one rental transaction). Each column holds one field (Title, Customer Name, Phone, Address, Director, Actor, and so on). But notice something: in this flat database you have to enter all the information each time for the database to do the things you want. That means each time a customer checks out a video you'd have to enter the renter's name, address, phone number, and all the information on the film as well. Your customers wouldn't put up with that for very long. What's more, when it came time to print those mailing labels, you'd have thousands of duplicates, one label for each time a customer rented a film. Flat databases are easy to design—but can be very inefficient to use. In this case, both you and your customers would quickly give up.

In a relational database, you avoid all this duplication by using more than one table. That may sound strange, but let's see how it works.

Your table to record transactions in a relational database looks something like the table shown in Figure 11-2.

Trans. No.	Date	VideoID	CustomerID	Returned
T0004	6/23/98	90003	1001	☑
T0005	6/23/98	90001	1005	☑
T0006	6/23/98	90006	1002	☐
T0007	6/24/98	90003	1005	☐
(AutoNumber)			0	0	☐

FIGURE 11-2

This table is used to store rental transactions only.

Notice how much simpler it is, just five columns—Transaction Number, Date, Video ID, Customer ID, and a Returned column to tell you if the video came back. But what about all the other information you want: customer names and addresses to create mailing labels, film information to track down that elusive Robert Mitchum movie, and your cost to buy the video for renting out? That's all stored in two other tables, as shown in Figures 11-3 and 11-4.

CustomerID	First Name	Last Name	Address	City	State	Postal Code	Home Phone
1001	Nancy	Davolio	507 - 20th Ave. E.	Seattle	WA	98122-	(206) 555-3487
1002	Janet	Leverling	722 Moss Bay Blvd.	Kirkland	WA	98033-	(206) 555-3497
1003	Andrew	Fuller	908 W. Capital Way	Tacoma	WA	98401-	(206) 555-3467
1004	Margaret	Peacock	4110 Old Redmond Rd.	Redmond	WA	98052-	(206) 555-3437
1005	Steven	Buchanan	14 Garrett Hill	Bellevue	WA	98010-	(425) 555-1212
(AutoNumber)							

FIGURE 11-3

This table stores customer information. Because you enter each customer's information only once, you save time and eliminate mistakes.

VideoID	Video Title	Price	Genre	Director	Lead Actor	Lead Actress
90001	Gone with the Wind	$49.99	Drama	Victor Fleming	Clark Gable	Vivian Leigh
90002	Die Hard	$29.99	Action	John McTiernan	Bruce Willis	Bonnie Bedelia
90003	Clockwork Orange, A	$34.99	Sci-Fi	Stanley Kubrick	Malcolm McDowell	
90004	Maltese Falcon, The	$29.99	Film Noir	John Huston	Humphrey Bogart	Mary Astor
90005	Night of the Hunter	$19.99	Film Noir	Charles Laughton	Robert Mitchum	Shelley Winters
90006	Herbie Goes Bananas	$79.99	Comedy	Vincent McEveety	Charles Martin Smith	Cloris Leachman
toNumber)		$0.00				

FIGURE 11-4

The table for information on each video in the store.

And those two tables are linked to the transaction table. In other words, the three tables work together, in relationship to each other. Thus, a "relational" database.

Notes *Access works a bit differently from other Office programs, such as Word or Excel. In the latter two, a **file** contains a single **document** or **workbook**. In Access, a single file can contain many **objects**—tables, **forms,** queries, and so forth, all working together.*

Now when you rent out a video, you enter only the Video ID number from the sticker you put on the tape and the Customer ID from the customer's membership card. That's it. (The program can add the transaction number and date automatically.) And when you want to send out a mailing list, there are no duplicates, because you entered each customer's name, address, and so on only once in the customer table. Looking for that Robert Mitchum movie? You could sort the video table by actor, or ask the database to find the information. (In database lingo, asking for information is called a query.)

Relational databases can be more complicated to design and build, but they save you enormous amounts of time and effort later when you're using them.

Using a Wizard to Create a New Database

Fortunately, Access gives you an easy way to design and build a relational database: using a Database Wizard.

 Notes   *As you become more familiar with Access, you might want to modify a database's structure or build one from scratch. You'll discover that Access has wizards to help you create individual objects (like tables) and even properties within an object.*

You can start a Database Wizard in two possible ways:

- When you start Access, it displays the **dialog box** shown in Figure 11-5. Simply **click** the Access Database Wizards, Pages, And Projects option button, and click OK.

FIGURE 11-5

The dialog box Access displays when you start the program.

- Or if you're already running Access, close any database you're working in and choose the File **menu's** New command, or click the New toolbar button.

Either way, Access displays the New dialog box. To create a database using a wizard, follow these steps:

1 Click the Databases tab to see a list of the wizards Access provides for the various types of databases, as shown in Figure 11-6.

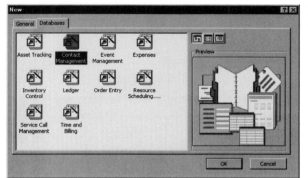

FIGURE 11-6

The Databases tab in the New dialog box.

2 Select the type of database you want to create, and click OK. For example, if you want to create a database to track contacts in your company, select Contact Management and click OK to display the File New Database dialog box.

3 Select a storage location for the database using the Save In drop-down list box.

4 Enter a name for the database in the File Name text box, and click Create. Access creates the database and displays the first Database Wizard dialog box, listing the type of information your database typically stores.

5 Click Next to start the wizard. The next dialog box displays a list of tables in your database, as shown in Figure 11-7. For each table it also shows the available fields.

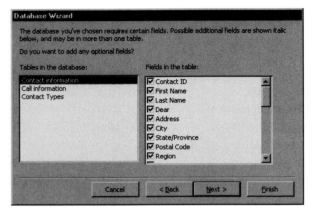

FIGURE 11-7

Adding fields to database tables.

6   Select a table name from the Tables In The Database list box, and then select or deselect fields for that table in the Fields In The Table list box.

7   Repeat step 6 for each table.

 Each field holds a certain kind of information, for example, first name, last name, company, address, and so forth.

 If Access asks you whether you want to include sample data in your new database, consider doing so. Including sample data helps you learn your way around your new database.

8   Click Next to choose a style for your database, as shown in Figure 11-8.

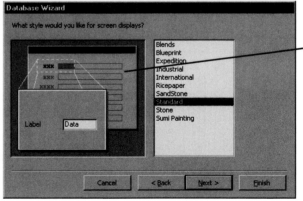

FIGURE 11-8

Selecting a database style.

A preview of the style.

The Standard design scheme might look dull, but its plain design makes data more readable than any other scheme.

9 Select a style name, and click Next to display the dialog box shown in Figure 11-9.

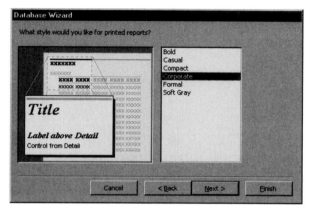

FIGURE 11-9

Choose a design scheme for your printed reports.

As with the previous design choices, simpler is probably better.

10 Select a design for your printed reports, and click Next. The wizard asks you to provide a title for the database, as shown in Figure 11-10. You can use the filename for the title, or you can enter a different name. The title appears on future reports you create.

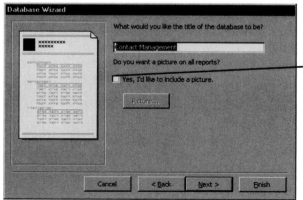

FIGURE 11-10

Enter a title to appear on all reports.

Select this check box to include a picture on reports.

11 Click Next to display the final dialog box, which confirms that you want to start working on the database as soon as the wizard builds it.

12 Click Finish, and the wizard builds your database. When it's finished, your screen looks something like the one shown in Figure 11-11.

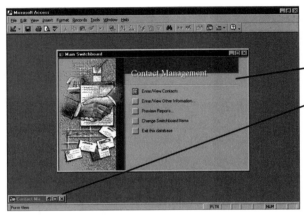

FIGURE 11-11

Your database's opening window.

The Switchboard is open and ready to go.

The Database Window is minimized.

The Switchboard is a menu system for quickly and easily performing common tasks in your database—like entering data. The Database Window is the command center for your entire database. You use the Database Window to access any of the database's objects—tables, queries, forms, reports, and so forth. In the next few sections, we'll explore using the Switchboard and Database Window to add, edit, delete, and otherwise manipulate data in your database.

 A quick inspection of the Database Window will show that there are three additional types of objects: pages, macros, and modules. A discussion of these objects is beyond the scope of this book. See your user documentation for more information.

Adding and Updating Information in Your Database

Now that you've created a database, you want use it, right? Since the primary purpose of a database is to store, manipulate, and retrieve information, you first need to add your information. This section describes how to add and delete data.

If you told Access to include sample data, you might want to play with the data for a while to get a sense of how the database works, and then delete the sample data before you load your own data. Once you've loaded, say, 500 names and addresses, it's much more difficult to find and delete sample data.

There are two ways you can enter data: directly into tables or by using a form. Both ways have their advantages and disadvantages. Let's look at using forms first.

Entering and Updating Data Using a Form

Typically the top button in your Switchboard is labeled Enter/View. There may be several Enter/View buttons, each for entering a different type of data. When you click the appropriate button, Access displays a form. Figure 11-12 shows a form for entering contact information, such as a sales person might use. The form currently shows information on a contact named Nancy Davolio.

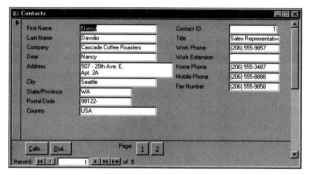

FIGURE 11-12

A form for entering contact information.

The Access form looks a lot like printed forms that you and I fill out all the time. That's one of the biggest advantages to using a form to add or look at data—its familiarity. By the way, all the data in this form belongs to a single record (a single row in a table). Each field in the form corresponds to a single field (a single column in a table).

To enter data, press the Tab, Enter, or arrow keys to move from field to field as you type the data. To change data in a field, move to the field and type the new data. (You don't have to delete the old data first.) To delete data from a field, move to the field and press the Delete key. It's as simple as that.

You can also select a field in which to enter data by clicking it. This is handy if you want to enter or change data in just a single field of a form.

 When it comes to the Save command, Access differs from other Office programs such as Word or Excel. Those programs save only when you tell them to. Access saves your data as soon as you enter it.

Figure 11-13 shows the series of buttons (on a form like this they're called controls) found at the bottom of the form. Table 11-1 explains their function (from left to right).

FIGURE 11-13

Use these buttons to move from record to record or begin a new record.

Control	Function
First Record	Moves to the first record in the database.
Previous Record	Moves to the previous record.
Current Record	Displays the number of the record you are currently viewing.
Next Record	Moves to the next record in the database.
Last Record	Moves to the last record in the database.
New Record	Creates a new record.

TABLE 11-1: Record navigation controls.

There are three ways to delete an entire record: you can choose the Edit menu's Delete Record command, click the Delete Record **toolbar** button, or click the vertical bar on the left side of the form and press the Delete key. When Access asks for confirmation, click Yes.

 Once you delete a record, you can't undo the delete; the record and all of its data are gone for good.

This particular form has a few interesting wrinkles. Near the bottom of the form are several buttons. The first one, Calls, displays a subform, as shown in Figure 11-14, that lists all the calls you've made to Nancy (or at least the ones you've entered in the database).

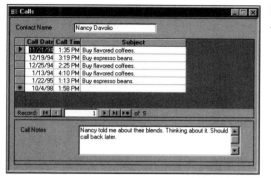

FIGURE 11-14

The Calls subform.

The second button, Dial, allows you to dial Nancy, if you've set up your phone to work through your computer.

Finally, there's the label Page, with the buttons marked 1 and 2. In this form, each record has so much information that to make things neater Access spreads the information across two pages. If you click 2, Access displays the Contacts form window shown in Figure 11-15. You can also get to the second page by scrolling down.

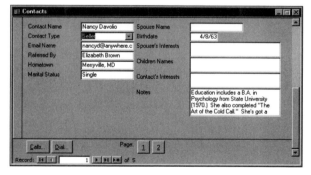

FIGURE 11-15

The second page of this form includes additional information on the same record.

Note that the contact name "Nancy Davolio" is repeated on the second page.

Forms can be a convenient, powerful way to enter and update data in your database. But sometimes you might want to enter data directly into the table.

Entering and Updating Data in a Table

There are several reasons you might want to bypass forms and work right in the table. You might have to update data in one field across many records—for example, if the boss decrees that from now on all salutations in mass mailings must be the more formal "Dear Ms. Davolio" and not "Dear Nancy," or if your city gets a new area code. In both cases, you could simply move down the Dear or Work Phone column and make the changes one after another, as shown in Figure 11-16.

	ID	First Name	Last Name	Dear	Title	Company Name	Address	Ci
⊞	1	Nancy	Davolio	Nancy	Sales Representative	Cascade Coffee Roasters	507 - 20th Ave. E.	Seattl
⊞	2	Janet	Leverling	Janet	Vice President, New Products	Northwind Traders	722 Moss Bay Blvd.	Kirkla
⊞	3	Andrew	Fuller	Andrew	Sales Representative	Volcano Coffee Company	908 W. Capital Way	Tacon
⊞	4	Margaret	Peacock	Margaret	Purchase Manager	Fourth Coffee	4110 Old Redmond Rd.	Redm
⊞	5	Steven	Buchanan	Steve	Purchase Manager	Health Food Store	14 Garrett Hill	Londo
▶	)er)							

FIGURE 11-16

A portion of the Contacts table displaying the same data as the forms previously shown.

To enter data, simply press the Tab, Enter, or arrow keys to move from field to field (and/or record to record) and then enter your data. To change data in a field, move to the field and type the new data. (You don't need to delete the old data first if it's highlighted.) To delete data from a field, move to the field and press the Delete key. It's just like working with forms.

You can create a new record in three different ways: choose the Insert menu's New Record command, click the New Record toolbar button, or move to the bottom of the table, to the blank record line, and begin entering data.

 It's common for database tables to include some kind of ID field, a unique identifier for each record. This ID field often uses the AutoNumber feature. If that's the case, move to the next field over and begin entering data—Access automatically supplies a sequential number.

To delete an entire record, follow these steps:

1 Select the entire row by clicking the row marker—the gray rectangle on the far left side of the row. This highlights the row.

2 You now have three choices: choose the Edit menu's Delete Record command, click the Delete Record toolbar button, or press the Delete key.

3 When Access asks if you really want to delete the record, click Yes.

 Once you delete a record, you can't undo the delete; the record and all its data are gone for good.

You may prefer entering and updating data directly into the table on a regular basis. For some people this method is faster. But there is one big disadvantage to this method: If your database has more than just a few fields, you can see only a small fraction of the total data in a record at one time. Most of the fields extend off the screen to the right. You can scroll to the right to see these other fields, but as certain fields (like the contact's name) scroll off to the left, it quickly becomes difficult to tell which record belongs to which contact.

Fortunately, Access has a solution. You can freeze one or more columns so they don't scroll off the screen. To do this, follow these steps:

1 Right-click the column heading of the column you want to freeze.

2 Choose the shortcut menu's Freeze Columns command.

Access moves the column you froze to the far left side. Figure 11-17 shows what the table looks like after freezing the First Name and Last Name fields and then scrolling over to the far right end of the table.

First Name	Last Name	Spouse Name	Spouse's Inter	Children Name	Hometown	Contact's Inter
⊞ Nancy	Davolio				Merryville, MD	
⊞ Janet	Leverling	Jim	Tennis, golf		San Francisco,	
⊞ Andrew	Fuller				Orlando, FL	
⊞ Margaret	Peacock	Brad	Biking, cross tra		Boston, MA	
⊞ Steven	Buchanan				London, UK	

FIGURE 11-17

A different portion of the Contacts table, with the contact's First Name and Last Name fields frozen.

To unfreeze the columns, choose the Format menu's Unfreeze All Columns command.

Querying Your Database

Whether you use forms or tables to enter your data in your database, that's just the beginning. A database really starts to work for you when you work with, or manipulate, the data. In this section, we'll look at how queries help you work with your data. The next section describes how reports help you look at your data.

Query is just another word for "question." When you query your database, you're asking it a question, like "Who are all our customers that live in Florida?" or "Who are all our customers in Florida that bought more than $1,000 in products last month?" You can query one or more tables; you can even query other queries.

Just as it has wizards for helping you build a database, Access also has wizards to help you build queries. Let's look at a database for a health-food store, and build a simple query.

 A simple query is also called a select query, because you select which data to display in the query.

To build a simple query, follow these steps:

1 Open the Database Window, and click the Queries button on the Objects bar, as shown in Figure 11-18.

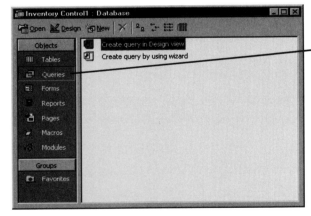

FIGURE 11-18

The Database Window.

Click the button on the Objects bar that corresponds to the type of object you want to work with.

2 Click the New toolbar button to display the New Query dialog box.

3 Select Simple Query Wizard from the list, as shown in Figure 11-19, and click OK.

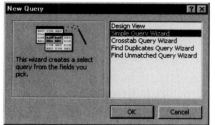

FIGURE 11-19

The New Query dialog box.

4 Use the dialog box shown in Figure 11-20 to select the fields you want to include in the query. Select the table containing the field you want to include from the Tables/Queries drop-down list box, and then select the fields you want to include from the table by ~~s~~ from the Available Fields list box and clicking ~~rrow~~ button. In the example, I select from two ~~for the product name) and Inventory Transac-~~ ~~rent unit price). By the way, I created this data-~~ ~~ventory Control Wizard.~~

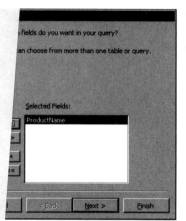

FIGURE 11-20

Select which fields you want included in the query.

the wizard asks whether you want a detail or ~~ry,~~ click the Detail option button to show every field ~~g records or click the Summary option button to~~ calculate and show a summary amount instead of the actual data for the fields you select. If you select Summary, click Summary Options to specify the fields for which you want to display a summary and what calculation you want to use for the summary. In this example, I'm using a detail query.

6 Click Next, and enter a name for your query. Then specify whether you want to run it or modify the design. When you're done, click Finish. Access displays the query results, as shown in Figure 11-21.

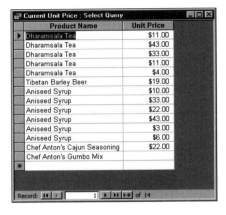

FIGURE 11-21

The query results.

Notes *To tabulate data in two different ways simultaneously, you need to create a crosstab query. For example, in our health-food store example, you could summarize sales by both product and date. Unlike a simple query, where you can gather data from multiple tables or queries, you can create a crosstab query from only a single table or query. You might need to create a simple query first to collect all the fields you want and then make the crosstab query off that simple query. When you run the Crosstab Query Wizard, you select the fields you want to use for row and column headings. Then you select the number you want calculated in boxes—the intersection of each row and column. Crosstab queries are powerful tools and can often be complex. You should probably gain some experience building simple queries before attempting a crosstab.*

Reporting on Database Information

Ultimately, you'll probably want to print reports for others to view. You can generate reports from tables or queries. Access gives you three ways to generate reports: using report wizards, using the **AutoReport** feature (a sort of one-click way to get a report fast), and designing reports yourself from scratch. This section shows you how to use the Report Wizard and AutoReport features.

Using AutoReport

AutoReport is the easiest way to create reports, so we'll start with that. To create a report using the AutoReport feature, follow these steps:

1   Open the Database Window, and click the Reports button on the Objects bar.

2   Click the New toolbar button to display the New Report dialog box.

3   Select AutoReport: Columnar or AutoReport: Tabular, as shown in Figure 11-22. The box on the left gives a rough idea of how these two forms look.

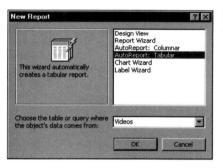

FIGURE 11-22

The New Report dialog box.

4   Select the table or query on which you want to base the report from the drop-down list box.

5   Click OK.

Access uses the design scheme you chose when you set up the database to create the report. The downside of AutoReport is that you have virtually no control over the design of the report as you're creating it. The only way to control how the reports look is to manually modify the design (see the end of the next section for a brief discussion).

Using the Report Wizard

To create a report using a wizard, follow these steps:

1   Open the Database Window, and click the Reports button on the Objects bar.

2   Click the New toolbar button to display the New Report dialog box.

3   Select Report Wizard from the list.

4 Select the table or query on which you want to base the report.

5 Click OK.

6 In the Report Wizard dialog box shown in Figure 11-23, select the fields you want in the report. Click a field, and then click the single right-arrow button. If you make a mistake and include a field you don't want, remove it by clicking the single left-arrow button. If you want all fields, click the double right-arrow button. Then click Next.

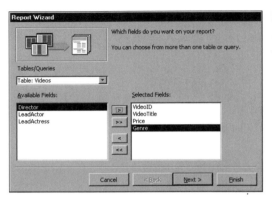

FIGURE 11-23

Choose which fields to include in the report.

7 Use the wizard's next dialog box, as shown in Figure 11-24, to select grouping levels for the information in the report. Select fields you want to group by, and click the single right-arrow button. You can also change priorities by clicking the down and up Priority arrows. When you've organized the information the way you want, click Next.

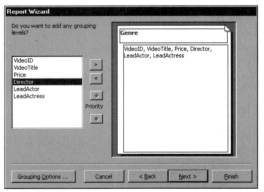

FIGURE 11-24

Choose the fields by which you want to group the report.

8 Use the wizard's next dialog box, as shown in Figure 11-25, to specify the sorting order of the records in the report. You can sort by up to four fields, in ascending or descending order. In this example, the videos will be sorted alphabetically by director, and within each director's group the videos will be sorted by title. After you determine your sort order, click Next.

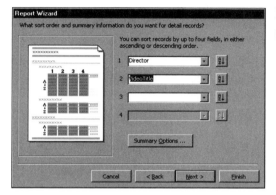

FIGURE 11-25

Sorting records in the report.

9 Select a layout for your report using the dialog box shown in Figure 11-26. When you select an option, the wizard displays a rough preview of how the report will look using that option. After you've selected a layout, click Next.

 If you have a lot of fields, you might want to select the landscape option under Orientation.

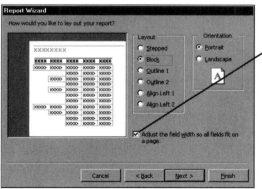

FIGURE 11-26

Selecting a report layout.

Select this check box to adjust field widths so all fields fit on one page.

10 Select a style for the report using the dialog box shown in Figure 11-27. Access provides six different styles of report from which to choose. Try them out, remembering that simpler is usually better. When you're finished, click Next.

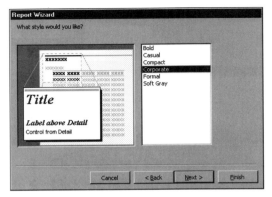

FIGURE 11-27

Selecting a report style.

11 In the wizard's last dialog box, enter a name for the report. You can choose to preview the report or modify its design. Click Finish, and you're done.

If you want to alter a report you've created, you need to view the report in Design **view.** Click the Design View toolbar button to display a schematic representation of the report and a special toolbar for modifying the design. How this all works is beyond the scope of this book, but if you play around a bit, you'll probably be able to make simple modifications.

 *The two basic building blocks of a report are **labels** (identifying the type of data) and **text boxes** (containing the data itself). Clicking labels or text boxes brings up selection handles that allow you to stretch, shrink, or move the selected element. You'll quickly see that modifying a report's design can be time-consuming, if not particularly difficult.*

APPENDIX A

Installing Office 2000

Installing Microsoft Office 2000 is easier than it was with previous versions of Microsoft Office. When you install Office 2000, you can choose to have the installation **program** take care of just about everything for you, or you can specify exactly what you want to install. You can even specify not to install features until you need to use them for the first time, freeing up hard disk space that you would've wasted with unused features or programs.

This appendix covers the following installation topics:

- Installing Office 2000 the first time
- Using Office 2000's Maintenance Mode

Installing Office 2000 the First Time

To install Microsoft Office 2000, close any programs you might have open and turn off any virus-checking programs you have. Then follow these steps:

1 Insert the Microsoft Office 2000 CD-ROM into your CD-ROM drive.

2 When the message box appears asking you to enter your customer information, enter your name, initials, and, if appropriate, your organization. Then enter the really long string of numbers and letters called your CD Key, which is located on the Office 2000 CD-ROM case. **Click** Next when you're finished.

 Do not lose your CD Key. If you lose this number, you won't be able to reinstall Office if you ever need to.

3 In the next screen, check to make sure your name is correct, choose the Accept The Terms In The License Agreement option, and click Next.

You can go back at any point before clicking Finish and change your settings in a previous screen. To do this, click Back.

4   Click Install Now to install the most frequently used features, and upgrade a previous version of Office, if you have one. Otherwise, to customize the installation procedure, click Customize (see Figure A-1).

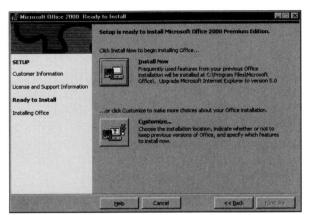

FIGURE A-1

Choosing the type of install to perform.

5   Click Next. If you chose Install Now, Office begins installing. Otherwise, the installation program continues.

6   Enter the name of the **folder** where you want to install Office, or click Browse to find the folder. Click Next.

7   Select an upgrade option for Internet Explorer from the drop-down list box, and then click Next.

8   Use the Select Features screen to select which Office programs and features you want to install (see Figure A-2). Click a plus sign to show additional features, and click the icons to display a list of installation options, as shown in Table A-1.

9   Click Upgrade Now (or Finish) to begin installing Office.

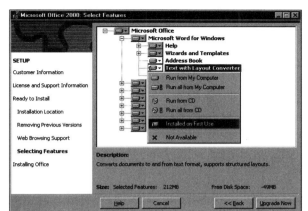

Installation Option	What It Does
Run From My Computer	Installs the feature or program to your hard drive.
Run All From My Computer	Installs all of the features in the category or program you selected to your hard drive.
Run From CD	Runs the feature or program from your CD-ROM drive. The Office CD-ROM must be in the drive.
Run All From CD	Runs all of the features in the category or program you selected from your CD-ROM drive.
Installed On First Use	Prompts you to install the feature or program the first time you attempt to use it.
Not Available	You cannot use the feature or program without running the Office 2000 Maintenance Mode and installing the feature.

TABLE A-1: Custom installation options.

*When you first launch **Microsoft Outlook 2000**, you use the Outlook Startup **Wizard** to configure Outlook for your **e-mail** services. Chapter 6 describes how to use the Outlook Startup Wizard.*

Using Office 2000's Maintenance Mode

After you have installed Office, you can change or repair your installation at any point by running the Office Maintenance Mode. To do this, follow these steps:

1 Click the Start button, point to Settings, and click Control Panel.

2 **Double-click** the Add/Remove Programs icon.

3 Select Microsoft Office 2000 from the list of installed programs, and then click Add/Remove.

4 After the Office Maintenance Mode program starts, click the option button corresponding to the action you want to take (see Figure A-3):

- Click Repair Office to fix any problems with Office.

- Click Add Or Remove Features to change the features you want to install or remove from your computer.

- Click Remove Office to completely remove Office from your computer.

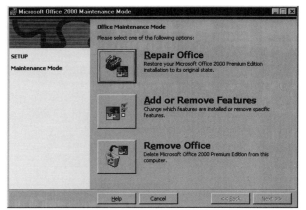

FIGURE A-3

The Office Maintenance Mode program.

5 If you chose to repair the installation, click an option button to specify whether you want to reinstall Office or repair errors, as shown in Figure A-4.

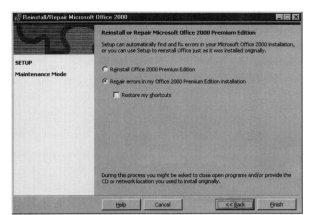

6 Click Finish to begin repairing Office 2000.

APPENDIX B

Glossary

Access; see Microsoft Access 2000

Animation Animation adds movement to text or a graphic. For example, in Word you can add a blinking background to text, and in PowerPoint you can animate the portions of a slide so they appear one at a time.

Application Application is another word for **program**.

Argument An argument is a variable within a **function** that is assigned a value when the function is run. Excel uses arguments to calculate **formulas**. Arguments are commonly shown in parentheses.

Attachment An attachment is any **file** or item that is attached to a message or document but is not actually a part of the document, much as a cover page may be paper-clipped to a document.

AutoContent Wizard PowerPoint's AutoContent Wizard helps you design and create a new presentation. Based on your answers to the AutoContent Wizard's questions, the wizard creates placeholder content in the presentation.

AutoCorrect AutoCorrect, a feature that corrects misspellings as you type, is available in all Office programs except Outlook.

AutoLayout If you create a blank presentation in PowerPoint, you can choose an AutoLayout for a slide. An AutoLayout includes place-holders for content such as clip art, text, and **tables**.

AutoReport The AutoReport feature in Access allows you to quickly create reports based on the report preferences you selected when setting up the database.

AutoSum AutoSum is a function of Excel that adds the values of a selected **range**. To add a column of numbers, select their cell range and click the AutoSum button. Excel places the sum of the numbers below the selected range.

AutoText   AutoText is a feature that lets you store text and then enter it in a document with a couple of keystrokes.

Bookmark   A bookmark is a named location in a document that you can use to quickly jump to a specific location.

Cell   A cell is the rectangular box in a **table** or **spreadsheet** where a row and a column intersect. Excel can divide worksheets into thousands of cells. Each cell has an address, which consists of its column letter and row number. For example, the cell where column B and row 2 meet is called cell B2.

Cell reference   A cell reference is an expression that defines a selected **range** of cells. For example (A1:A4) is a cell reference for the range of cells from A1 to A4.

Cell selector   The cell selector is the bold border that Excel uses to mark the active cell. To move the cell selector, click a different cell or use the arrow keys.

Channel   A channel is a **web site** that the web site publisher configures in a manner that allows people to download it using Internet Explorer. To view a list of channels, click Internet Explorer's Favorites toolbar button and then click the Channels folder.

Chart Wizard   Excel's Chart Wizard helps you create charts that visually portray data. To run Excel's Chart Wizard, choose the Insert menu's Chart command.

Chat; see Microsoft Chat

Click   The process of pointing to an item and then pressing and releasing the left mouse button is called clicking the item.

Click-and-Type   Click-and-Type is a new feature in Word 2000 that lets you enter text or a picture anywhere on the page, not just at the **insertion point**. To use Click-and-Type, you must be in Print Layout or Web Layout view. Simply double-click where you want to enter text or a picture.

Client   A client is a program that runs on your computer and works in tandem with a server program running on another server computer.

ClipArt Gallery   The ClipArt Gallery is a collection of pictures, sound clips, and movie clips that comes with Office. You can insert any clip art item in any Office program.

Clipboard The Windows Clipboard stores whatever object (a block of text, a picture, or even an entire folder) you copy or cut until you paste the object or copy or cut another object. The Office Clipboard keeps a maximum of the last 12 items you copy or cut from an Office program. You use the Clipboard toolbar to insert any one of the items or all the items at one time.

Connection Wizard The Connection Wizard is a program you can use to set up your Internet connection. To use the Connection Wizard, double-click the Connect To The Internet icon on your desktop, or click the Start button, point to Programs, Accessories, and Internet Tools, and then click Connection Wizard. Follow the instructions to set up an Internet connection.

Contacts Outlook's Contacts folder lets you store contact information for people: their e-mail and street addresses, phone numbers, and so forth.

Copy The Copy function allows you to create exact duplicates of text or images and store them on the Clipboard. You can copy an item by selecting it and pressing Ctrl+C. Or you can select the item and click the Copy toolbar button.

Cube A cube is a three-dimensional **range** in an Excel workbook. When you select a range of cells in an Excel worksheet and then select a range from another worksheet, you are selecting a cube.

Cursor A cursor is the small arrow, hourglass, pointing hand, or other symbol that moves on your screen as you move the mouse. Cursors are also the blinking vertical bars or other indicators that mark where the next character will appear when you begin typing.

Cut You cut a selection to move the selection to the Clipboard for pasting in another location. To cut an item, select the item and press Ctrl+X or select the item and click the Cut toolbar button.

Database A database is a type of **file** used for holding records.

Data category A data category organizes the values in a chart's data series. For example, a chart that plots changes over time has a data category of time.

Data point A data point is an individual statistic, fact, or piece of information that you can enter in a **cell** in Excel.

Data series A data series is a string of related values you plot together to analyze them and locate a pattern. For example, a line chart shows a data series plotted on a line.

Data source A data source is a list of information such as names, addresses, and the like.

Design template Design template is PowerPoint's and Publisher's term for what the other Office programs refer to as a **document template**.

Dialog box A dialog box is a special kind of window. Unlike other windows, you can usually display only one dialog box at a time. To work in another window, you must first close the dialog box.

Digital ID A digital ID is a small piece of code that you can obtain from a security vendor, such as Verisign, Inc. A digital ID provides a digital verification of your identity, most often to create a digital signature for an e-mail message.

Digital signature A digital signature is a special type of mark that can be applied to e-mail messages to verify that the message is a legitimate message from the stated sender. In order to create a digital signature, you must have a digital ID.

Document The kind of **file** you create with a word processor is called a document. The term *document file* refers more generally to any type of file you create using a program. The Start menu's Documents folder, for instance, contains the list of document files you last worked on.

Document template A document template is a partially completed document. It usually contains formatting and sometimes contains text and other information. Office programs provide document templates to save you time.

Document window The document window is the window within a program window in which you create a document file.

Double chevron The double chevron is a symbol that looks like two greater-than symbols: >>.

Double-click The process of pointing to an item and quickly clicking the left mouse button two times is called double-clicking the item.

Drag Dragging involves pressing the left mouse button, holding down the button while moving the mouse, and then releasing the button. You can drag to move objects to a new location or to draw objects with the Drawing tools.

E-mail   An e-mail message is an electronic message, usually in the form of text, which you send from one computer to another.

Excel; see Microsoft Excel 2000

Favorites   The Favorites folder is a special folder that you can use to hold shortcuts to **web pages** and files that you want to be able to find easily.

File   A file is what Windows stores on your computer's storage devices—devices such as hard disks, floppy disks, and sometimes CD-ROMs. There are two types of files: document files store the information you create with a program such as a word processor; program files contain the instructions your computer needs to perform tasks.

File extension   A file extension indicates a file's type, such as a program file you can run, a text file, or a certain type of image file. A file extension is the character sequence (usually three letters long) after the period in a file's name.

Folder   Windows stores the **files** on your computer's storage devices in folders. When you open or save a file, you can retrieve it from or place it in a folder that's listed in the Places bar, or you can select or create another folder in which to store it.

Font   Font determines what the text you type looks like. Some fonts are plain; others are flashy. Windows comes with many fonts you can use with Word and other Office programs.

Form   Forms are parts of documents or entire documents that contain boxes for people to fill in online. Many **web pages** have forms. You can create forms in Office programs using the Forms toolbar.

Formula   A formula is a rule or a principle expressed by algebraic symbols. Excel allows you to use formulas to calculate algebraic functions. For help creating **functions**, use the Formula Wizard. To run the Formula Wizard, click the toolbar's Function Wizard button.

Frame   A frame is a square or rectangular section of a page. **Web pages** are often divided into separate rectangular frames, which can display information or perform functions. You can select a frame within a web page by clicking it. In Publisher, you use frames to work with the individual elements of the publication: pictures, blocks of text, and so forth.

B

Free/Busy information Free/Busy information is the calendar information that Outlook posts to your network or **web site** so other users can schedule appointments with you. Free/Busy information shows only the times in your Calendar when you are free or busy; it does not reveal other information about your appointments.

FrontPage Express; see Microsoft FrontPage Express

Function Functions are **formulas** you can use to make calculations in Excel. You can enter functions in Excel by entering the arguments in the text boxes supplied in the Paste Function dialog box.

HTML HTML (HyperText Markup Language) is the standard document format for **web pages** and is an alternate file format for Office 2000 documents. HTML is popular because you can apply formatting to HTML documents and the formatting can be viewed almost universally, using a variety of common programs (such as **web browsers**).

Hyperlink A hyperlink is a piece of text or an image that points to another resource (usually on the Internet), such as a web page.

Insertion point The insertion point is a vertical, blinking bar that indicates the placement of the next character you type. It is also referred to as a **cursor**.

Internet The Internet is a global network of millions of single computers and smaller electronic networks. The Internet lets people across the world share information quickly and inexpensively, which is why the Internet is often referred to as the "information superhighway." A couple of the Internet's most popular services are electronic mail (e-mail) and the World Wide Web.

Internet Connection Wizard; see Connection Wizard

Internet Explorer; see Microsoft Internet Explorer 5

Intranet An intranet is an internal network that works like and uses the technology of the Internet.

Label A label is a cell entry that is not intended to be used in a **formula** or **function**. Labels are usually text or numbers that you enter into a worksheet to explain the meaning of the other figures in the worksheet.

Legend A legend is a table on a chart that shows the symbols used.

Link; see Hyperlink

Mail Merge   Mail Merge is a Word feature that you can use to combine a data source with other documents and can print envelopes, mailing labels, and form letters.

Menu   All Office programs have menus. Near the top of a program window is a row of words. The first word in the row is often File, and the last is often Help. These words are the names of the menus. Menus hold a set of commands for working with related tasks. If you click the word File, for example, you open the File menu, which holds several commands for working with files.

B

Microsoft Access 2000   Access is a relational **database** program. You can use Access to create multiple databases that you want to be able to work with in connection with one another.

Microsoft Chat   Microsoft Chat is an Internet Explorer component that allows you to participate in real-time Internet chat room discussions.

Microsoft Excel 2000   Excel is a **spreadsheet** program that you can use to do numeric analysis. You can use Excel to create and track budgets, perform statistical analysis, create charts, and much, much more.

Microsoft Exchange Server   Exchange Server is a messaging product that corporations frequently use for internal network **e-mail**. Outlook 2000 is specifically designed to work with Exchange Server, providing a number of features that can be used when sending messages to other users across an Exchange Server network.

Microsoft FrontPage Express   FrontPage Express is a mini-version of Microsoft FrontPage that comes with Internet Explorer. You can use FrontPage Express to create and edit **web pages**, but it lacks many of FrontPage's advanced web page– and web site–creation features.

Microsoft Internet Explorer 5   Internet Explorer is a **web browser** that you can use to view **web pages**, search the Internet, create and send e-mail, access newsgroups, video-conference, and chat.

Microsoft NetMeeting   NetMeeting is a conferencing program that you can use to share programs, collaborate on documents, draw on a whiteboard, chat using the keyboard, or meet with a group of people using voice or video.

Microsoft Outlook 2000   Outlook is a personal information manager that you can use to send and receive **e-mail**, manage tasks, keep an appointment calendar, and maintain an address book.

Microsoft Outlook Express   Outlook Express is a mini-version of Outlook that you can use to send and receive e-mail and create and maintain an address book. Outlook Express also lets you work with newsgroups and functions as Outlook's newsreader.

Microsoft PowerPoint 2000   PowerPoint is a program for creating presentations (slide shows) you can show on your computer, present in front of an audience with the help of a projector, or give over an intranet or the Internet. You can also use PowerPoint to create 35 mm slides, overhead transparencies, and printed handouts.

Microsoft Publisher 2000   Publisher is a desktop publishing program that simplifies the process of creating documents for publishing, documents that frequently have a more complex layout than most Word documents. With Publisher, you can quickly and easily create well-designed publications such as newsletters, catalogs, brochures, and even books.

Microsoft Windows   Windows is a family of operating systems that grew out of the original Windows program that ran on top of Microsoft's DOS operating system. The Windows family includes the now-discontinued Windows 3.1, and Windows 95, Windows 98, Windows NT, Windows 2000, and Windows CE. Although Windows 3.1 programs run on all other versions of Windows except Windows CE (which requires programs that have been specifically adapted to the Windows CE operating system), programs designed for the newer versions of Windows work best.

Microsoft Word 2000   Word is primarily a word processing program, but you can also use it to create **web pages** and to desktop-publish newsletters, brochures, and so forth.

NetMeeting; see Microsoft NetMeeting

Newsgroup   A newsgroup is a collection of messages—typically text messages—that people post to a central server so other people can read them. Newsgroup messages closely resemble **e-mail** messages—in fact, you use the same basic process to create and post a newsgroup message as you do to create and send an e-mail message.

Newsgroup reader A newsgroup reader, or newsreader, is any program that allows you to read and write messages on a newsgroup. Outlook Express is the newsgroup reader that comes with Windows, Internet Explorer, and Office.

Object In Office 2000, the term *object* means something you create in one program that you can insert in another program. Objects can be tables, charts, video clips, pictures, sound clips, graphics you create with the Drawing tools, or even entire Office documents, to name a few. You can insert almost any type of object in any Office program. Publisher has an even broader definition of the term *object:* an object is any item you work with, including those items that you create in Publisher (such as a frame of text), instead of just those items inserted from another program. Publisher's Objects toolbar lets you work with the various types of objects.

Office Assistant The Office Assistant is a graphical character that is part of the Office Help system. You can ask the Assistant questions or ask it to search on terms.

Offline page An offline page is a **web page** that you've told Internet Explorer to automatically download at certain intervals so you can view the page without connecting to the Internet.

Online Working online (as opposed to working offline) means that your Internet (or network) connection is open and ready for use.

Operating system An operating system (or OS) is the software on your computer that manages your computer's hardware and resources. Windows 95, Windows 98, Windows NT, and Windows 2000 are all operating systems, as is the Mac OS. Programs, such as the Office programs, are designed to work with particular operating systems.

Operator An operator is a symbol for expressing a mathematical function. For example, a plus sign or a minus sign.

Organization chart An organization chart is a chart that depicts a hierarchical organization. Organization charts are commonly inserted in PowerPoint presentations.

Outlook; see Microsoft Outlook 2000

Outlook Express; see Microsoft Outlook Express

Page orientation   In Office programs, you can print a page in portrait or landscape orientation. In portrait orientation, a page prints vertically; in landscape orientation, it prints horizontally.

Password   A password is a secret word or string of characters that you use to confirm your identity. When you log on to Windows, you may need to supply a name to identify yourself and a password to prove you're who you say you are.

Paste   The Paste function allows you to move text or images from the Clipboard to another document. To use the Paste function, place the pointer exactly where you would like to place the text or image. Right-click, and choose the shortcut menu's Paste command. Or you can paste by clicking the toolbar's Paste button or pressing Ctrl+V.

Path   The path to a file describes the file's location—the disk, the **folder**, and the subfolder in which the file is located.

Personal menu   Office programs create Personal menus to suit your personal computing needs. Over time, Office programs "learn" which tools you use most commonly and display them on your Personal menus.

Personal toolbar   Most of the Office 2000 programs allow you to combine the Standard and Formatting toolbars onto one line. This new single-line toolbar is called the Personal toolbar.

Places bar   The Open and Save As dialog boxes in the Office programs include a bar with shortcuts to commonly used storage locations, such as the My Documents folder, so you can quickly open or save to these locations.

Pop-up window   Office uses pop-up windows to display relevant information. They look like message boxes, but they don't have a title bar or a control menu.

PowerPoint; see Microsoft PowerPoint 2000

Presentation   In PowerPoint, a presentation is a collection of slides.

Program   As the term is used in this book, a *program* is a piece of software you use to perform your work or have fun with your computer. Each of the components in Office is a program.

Program window   The program window is the window containing the menu bar and toolbars used in the program. Unlike previous versions, Office 2000 opens multiple document files in their own program windows, instead of in separate document windows within the program window.

Publisher; see Microsoft Publisher 2000

Query   You query a **database** to ask the database for information that fits your criteria. Access has wizards that help you query various objects in a database to extract the information you need.

Range   A range is a specified area within a worksheet. To select a range, click the **cell** in the top left corner of the range and drag the mouse to the bottom right corner. Excel specifies a range by outlining the cells with a gray box and reversing the color within the cells.

Read-only   Read-only refers to a file that you can read or print but cannot edit.

Record   A record is a single entry in a database. Access stores information in records.

Ruler   The ruler is a visual tool that you can use to set margins, tabs, and indentations in an Office document.

Slide   In PowerPoint, slides are the components that make up a presentation. A slide can contain text, graphics, a chart, a table, and so on.

Source data table   A source data table is a table that displays the root information from which a chart is derived.

Spell checker   A spell checker is a tool that checks the spelling in a document.

Spreadsheet   A spreadsheet is a worksheet that contains mathematical information organized in rows and columns for the purpose of analysis and calculation. Excel is a spreadsheet program.

Style   A style is a collection of formats you can apply with a couple of mouse clicks and can include **fonts**, sizes, font attributes, alignment, character spacing, paragraph spacing, bullets and numbering, borders, indenting, and just about any other formatting you can think of. A *stylesheet* is a collection of styles.

Subfolder   A subfolder is a **folder** within a folder. Subfolders help you organize **files** within folders.

Suite   A suite is a set of software programs offered in a single package. The Microsoft Office 2000 Standard version contains the programs Excel, PowerPoint, Word, and Outlook.

Synchronize   You use Internet Explorer's Synchronize command to download the latest version of any offline pages you have set up, as well as changes to any web folders you have set up for offline viewing.

Table   A table is a format for presenting information in rows and columns. The rows and columns consist of **cells**, the places in a table where rows and columns intersect.

Template; see Document template

Text box   A text box is a box inserted in a document that can contain text or graphics set off for emphasis. For example, a text box might contain a headline or an announcement in the middle of a page.

Theme   Themes are preformatted design templates you can use to create **web pages**.

Toolbar   Some programs display rows of clickable buttons beneath their menu bars, which you can use to issue commands to a program. These rows of clickable buttons are called toolbars.

Transition   In PowerPoint, a transition is a special effect that occurs between **slides**.

URL   URL stands for uniform resource locator. A URL is an address for an Internet location.

Value   A value is a number you enter in a spreadsheet **cell**. A value can be used in a **formula**.

View   A view is the display of a document from a particular perspective. In Word, you can display a document in five views: Normal, Print Layout, Outline, Print Preview, and Full Screen. In PowerPoint, you can display a document in five views: Normal, Outline, Slide, Slide Sorter, and Slide Show. In Excel, you can display a document in five views: Normal, Page Break Preview, Full Screen, Print Preview, and Custom. Additionally, Word, PowerPoint, and Excel include a pseudo-view typically called Web Layout or Web Page Preview that lets you see how your document looks as a web page.

Web browser   A web browser is a program that lets you view **web pages** on the World Wide Web. Popular web browsers include Microsoft Internet Explorer and Netscape Navigator.

Web folder   A web folder is a **web site** using FrontPage or Office Server Extensions that you have set up for use with Office 2000. After you set up your web site as a web folder, you can treat it just like a folder on your hard drive.

Web page   A web page is a file that a business or individual publishes to the World Wide Web for other people to see. Web pages commonly include multimedia elements—such as pictures, text, and even sound. They also almost always include **hyperlinks** connecting them to other web pages.

Web site   A web site is a collection of web pages connected by **hyperlinks**. People and companies publish web sites on the World Wide Web when they have more information to share than will fit comfortably on one page. For example, a company web site might include one web page listing products and services, one listing employment opportunities, one with hyperlinks to the latest news releases, and so on.

Wildcard   When you search for a **file**, a block of text, or even a resource on the Internet, you can often use wildcards to take the place of one or more other characters. The most common wildcard is the asterisk (*).

Windows; see Microsoft Windows

Wizard   A wizard is a little program that steps you through a process by asking questions. It collects your answers and then produces, for example, a PowerPoint presentation or a fax cover sheet.

Word; see Microsoft Word 2000

WordArt   WordArt is a program you can use to create special text effects. For example, you can shape or wrap text, rotate it, give it a three-dimensional appearance, or place a shadow behind it.

Word processor   A word processor is a program that lets you create, save, and print text documents such as letters, school reports, and business documents. Word is a word processor.

Workbook   A workbook is a volume of records. Excel stores information in workbooks, which are divided into worksheets. You can save your workbooks on your hard drive, or you can save them on floppy disks.

B

World Wide Web   The World Wide Web, or Web for short, is the collection of web pages on the Internet that are interconnected by hyperlinks.

X-axis   The X-axis is the horizontal axis of a chart.

Y-axis   The Y-axis is the vertical axis of a chart.

Zip   Zip refers to two items. Zip drives are high-density removable floppy drives. Zip, the program, is a **file** compression utility that you can use to squeeze a file into a smaller space.

INDEX

INDEX

INDEX

INDEX